S0-BCI-257

The Complete Guide to
STONESCAPING

DRY-STACKING, MORTARING, PAVING & GARDENSCAPING

DAVID REED

LARK

An Imprint of Sterling Publishing
387 Park Avenue South
New York, NY 10016

Text © 2013 by David Reed
Illustrations © 2013, Lark Crafts, an Imprint of Sterling Publishing Co., Inc.
Photography © 2013 by David Reed unless otherwise specified

All rights reserved. No part of this publication may be reproduced, stored in a retrieval system,
or transmitted, in any form or by any means, electronic, mechanical, photocopying, recording, or
otherwise, without prior written permission from the publisher.

ISBN 978-1-4547-0387-7

Library of Congress Cataloging-in-Publication Data

Reed, David, 1957-
 [Works]
 The complete guide to stonescaping : dry-stacking, mortaring, paving & gardenscaping / David Reed.
   pages cm
 This book is comprised of materials from the following Lark Crafts and Sterling Publishing titles: The
Art & Craft of Stonework, ©2002 by David Reed. The Art & Craft of Stonescaping, ©1999 by David Reed.
 Includes bibliographical references and index.
 ISBN 978-1-4547-0387-7 (alk. paper)
 1. Garden structures--Design and construction--Amateurs' manuals. 2. Stonemasonry--Amateurs'
manuals. 3. Stone in landscape gardening. I. Reed, David, 1957- Art and craft of stonework. II. Reed,
David, 1957- Art and craft of stonescaping. III. Title.
 TH4961.R44 2013
 693'.1--dc23
                    2012042690

Distributed in Canada by Sterling Publishing
c/o Canadian Manda Group, 165 Dufferin Street
Toronto, Ontario, Canada M6K 3H6
Distributed in the United Kingdom by GMC Distribution Services
Castle Place, 166 High Street, Lewes, East Sussex, England BN7 1XU
Distributed in Australia by Capricorn Link (Australia) Pty. Ltd.
P.O. Box 704, Windsor, NSW 2756, Australia

For information about custom editions, special sales, and premium and corporate purchases, please
contact Sterling Special Sales at 800-805-5489 or specialsales@sterlingpublishing.com.

Email academic@larkbooks.com for information about desk and examination copies.
The complete policy can be found at larkcrafts.com.

Every effort has been made to ensure that all the information in this book is accurate. However, due
to differing conditions, tools, and individual skills, the publisher cannot be responsible for any injuries,
losses, and other damages that may result from the use of the information in this book.

Manufactured in China

2 4 6 8 10 9 7 5 3 1

larkcrafts.com

The Complete Guide to
STONESCAPING

PUBLIC LIBRARY
SEP   2013
SOUTH BEND, INDIANA

INTRODUCTION

Think stone. The sun-warmed, rough surface of a rock in your hand; snow-dusted boulders on a hillside. Magnificent Incan temples; abandoned campfires, ringed with blackened rocks. Glistening pebbles in a creek bed; stacked stone walls on a terraced Italian hillside. The megaliths at Stonehenge; the stepping-stone path to your garden. Our fascination with stone—its permanence and simplicity, its beauty and mystery—is as old and enduring as stone itself.

Stacking and laying stone are more popular today than ever. Why? In our high-tech world, stonescaping allows us the rare opportunity to reconnect with our natural surroundings. What's more, working with stone offers tangible, deeply satisfying, and lasting rewards. Walking past a stone structure you've built yourself is a pleasure like no other. Set three stones to make a garden bench or stack a small retaining wall—just a few feet long and a couple of feet high—and you'll know exactly what I mean.

All you need to start are rocks, gravel, a few basic tools, and this book. You don't have to be a male with arms of steel, a wealthy landowner with a huge estate, or an engineer with hundreds of specialized tools. If you can handle a shovel, wield a hammer, and lift small stones, and if you're eager to spend some time outdoors, the world of stonescaping is yours.

This book introduces you to many of the ways to build and decorate with stone. Whether you're thinking of building a wall, redesigning a garden, or simply seeking a new medium to express yourself, I'll take you through what you need to know to get started on your journey. Enjoy!

CHAPTER ONE

ALL ABOUT STONE

This chapter will not only familiarize you with the language of stonework, but also describe the characteristics and qualities to look for in stones, and where and how to find the stones for your project. Sometimes it's as easy as picking out stones from a pile at the stone yard. Other times, you may have to search around a bit. Either way, don't underestimate the creativity and joy involved in the hunt for the perfect stone.

Stones to Know

Though you probably had to memorize the three main types of rocks in school, chances are you don't remember how they're different from one another. Igneous rock is extremely dense and hard (examples are granite and basalt). Sedimentary rock, such as limestone and sandstone, is of medium-density and is relatively easy to work with. Metamorphic rock includes any kind of stone that has been transformed by heat, pressure, or chemical action into another type of stone, such as marble, which is altered limestone, or gneiss, which was once granite. Within these categories are many kinds of rock with names that may vary from one region to the next.

The chart below provides descriptions of suitable stones.

Thin fieldstones lend a rustic, layered look to a retaining wall.

Stone	Weight Relative to Size	Color	Grain	Workability	Strength
Basalt	Heavy	Grey to black, and brown	Fine	Moderate	Excellent
Gneiss	Medium	Grey to black, with bands of white quartz	Medium	Good	Good
Granite	Heavy	Pale grey to pale red	Medium to coarse	Difficult	Excellent
Limestone	Heavy	Pale green, grey, tan, white, black	Even	Moderate	Good to excellent
Sandstone	Medium (dense)	Grey to brown	Even grain	Good	Good to excellent
Slate	Medium	Black, blue, dark grey	Fine	Good	Good for paving

Weathered, dimensional blocks of *granite* make this covered niche an inviting spot to sit.

Stone carver Tom Jackson renders architectural features from Indiana limestone. The consistency of this oolitic limestone makes it a predictable material to carve.

Though not a list of every stone imaginable, what follows is a list of common stones and brief descriptions of each. This will help you determine the kind of stone you want to use for your projects and what's available in your area.

Alabaster: This dense translucent or white fine-grained gypsum is slightly harder than soapstone and great for carving.

Argillite: This metamorphic rock is of medium to hard density (somewhere between shale and slate) and dark red in color. It's used for building, and it's usually cut into blocky, rectangular and square shapes.

Basalt: This is a dark-colored, fine-grained igneous rock formed by the solidification of lava. There are many types of basalt distributed throughout the world. The Giants Causeway, located along the coast of Northern Ireland, is made up of an estimated 37,000 basalt columns, ranging from polygons to hexagons.

Also found in the United States' Pacific Northwest, basalt is often used in water features and as water basins.

Feldspar: This rock-forming mineral occurs mostly in igneous rocks, and nearly 60 percent of the Earth's crust is composed of it.

Gneiss: This metamorphic rock is made up of separate layers or bandings of materials, such as quartz, feldspar, and mica. With its rustic surface quality, gneiss is a good building stone for mortared veneer and dry stone walls and can commonly be found on mountainous slopes, in fields, and in creek beds.

Granite: Often used in building and ornamental work, this heavy, coarse-grained igneous rock contains quartz and feldspar. It's one of the hardest and most durable stones.

Hornblende: This is a bluish green to black mineral found in newly formed igneous rock.

Limestone: Primarily made of calcium carbonate derived from marine sediments, this sedimentary stone is good for carving and building. Varieties of limestone include oolitic, dolomitic, and carboniferous, each distinguished from one another by texture and density.

Marble: This is a fine- to coarse-grained, crystalline rock, such as limestone, which has metamorphosed from its original form by heat and pressure.

Quartz: This is a common mineral consisting primarily of silica, a compound of silicon and oxygen. Quartz is present in many rocks and appears as speckling in granite and as bands in stones such as gneiss and hornblende.

Quartzite: This is metamorphosed sandstone that's extremely hard and nonporous. It contains up to 90 percent quartz. Though considered a hard stone, it tends to shatter when struck with a hammer. Quartzite makes a good border around garden beds, and larger weathered pieces make interesting viewing stones.

Sandstone: This is a porous sedimentary stone with a consistent crystalline structure. Sandstone of medium density is an excellent choice for mortared and dry-laid stonework. It's easy to break and trim with a hammer, and it's also suitable for stone carving.

Schist: This is a metamorphic rock composed of flaky, relatively parallel layers of minerals, including iron and mica.

Shale: This is a soft rock composed of layers of compacted, fine-grained clay, silt, or mud sediments.

Slate: This metamorphic rock was fine clay that has been metamorphosed by heat and pressure. This dense, fine-grained stone readily splits into thin, smooth pieces commonly used for roofing, mortared paving, and kitchen countertops.

Soapstone: This is a soft, metamorphic rock composed mostly of talc. It has a smooth, soapy feel, and it's great for carving.

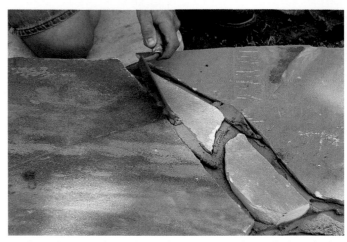

Medium-density split sandstone has a gritty surface, which is ideal for mortared or dry-laid paving.

The Language of Stone

Before visiting your local stone yard or stone supplier, familiarize yourself with the terms stonemasons use. It'll make discussing what you're looking for a whole lot easier, and professionals tend to appreciate amateurs who know what they're talking about before wandering into a stone yard. Also, refer to this glossary as you're reading this book.

Aggregate: This is a common term describing crushed, sharp-edged quarried stone, such as ⅜-inch (1 cm) pea gravel and larger pieces up to 1½ inches (3.8 cm), used in concrete mixtures and road bond. Larger aggregate, such as railroad ballast, is 2½ inches (6.4 cm) in size and makes a good base for paths in damp, boggy soil. It's also good for filling in driveway potholes.

Anchors (or deadmen): These are long stones that are set randomly into retaining walls, with their lengths positioned across, rather than along, the length of the wall. Because their back ends extend into the gravel backfill, they anchor the wall.

Large pieces of fieldstone make substantial capstones for this dry-stacked retaining wall.

An even row of neatly stacked single coping stones.

Carefully selected cornerstones are used here to make a stout stone post at a wall's end.

Ashlar: This is quarried stone that has been cut to specific dimensions and laid in deliberate patterns with consistent mortar joints.

Berm: This is a raised bank of soil. It can also be a mound of earth placed against the wall of a building to provide protection or insulation.

Bond stones: These are stones that break vertical joints and extend well into a wall in order to give structural integrity to stonework.

Boulder: A boulder is simply any rock that's too heavy for one peron to lift by hand.

Capstones: These are the uppermost stones on a wall (laid horizontally). They're used to finish a wall and protect the stonework.

Chinking stones: These are small stones or broken pieces that are used to fill in gaps in wide joints between larger stones.

Coping stones: These are the uppermost stones on a wall, most often set on top of the capstone course. Used on both freestanding and retaining walls, these stones are set vertically in a series that's either plumb or at a slight angle (around 15°).

Corbel: This is a cantilevered stone supported at only one end. It's often stacked two or more on top of one another, stepping out as they rise.

This dressed, dimensional stone laid in an ashlar pattern has a bold, rough-pitched surface that complements the size of the stone.

Most stone yards will have bulk piles of building stone, such as this selection of fieldstone.

Cornerstones: Stacked at wall ends and set at outside corners of coursed stonework, these stones have two faces 90° from each other.

Courses: These are the horizontal layers of stones in any mortared or dry-stacked stone wall.

Crushed stone: This is quarried stone, such as pea gravel or larger aggregates.

Dimensional stone: This is stone that's quarried and cut to an exact size and shape. Granite, marble, and limestone are common dimensional stones used in architectural stonework.

Dressed stone: This is dimensional stone that has had a particular texture, motif, or pattern worked on the stone's face.

Face: A stone's face is the surface chosen to be exposed when set into vertical stonework, such as a wall.

Fieldstones: These are stones found loose on the ground or embedded in the soil. They often appear mysteriously each spring as the frozen ground pushes them to the surface. You can use fieldstones as stepping stones, pavers, and wall stones. Weathered fieldstone is preferred in most cases, particularly for boulderscaping and stones set in Japanese-style gardens.

Flagstone: Also referred to as flagging, a flagstone is any stone used for paving, including fieldstone, random or cut sandstone, and slate.

Glacial erratics: These are stones that have wandered from their place of origin by way of glacial movement.

Gravel (washed crushed stone): This is ⅜- to 1½- inch (1 to 3.8 cm) crushed stone.

Hearting: The process of filling the core of a dry-stacked wall with small stones and rock chips until every space is packed tightly.

Igneous rock: This is a rock formed from reservoirs of molten lava made up of crystallized minerals. It solidifies at the Earth's surface or by extreme pressure below the Earth. Granite is the preeminent igneous rock, noted for its hardness and lasting qualities.

Joint: A joint is the space between any two stones in a stone structure. There are horizontal joints between courses of stonework and vertical joints between stones in each course.

Metamorphic rock: This is stone that was originally igneous or sedimentary but has changed in appearance and character through the natural forces of heat, pressure, and water. Granite could become gneiss; limestone

Smooth, rounded stones, referred to as river slicks, are used to dress up paving projects and water features, adding interesting colors and textures.

One-ton (0.9 t) wire baskets of building stone in a stone yard.

could recrystallize into marble; shale might be transformed by pressure into slate.

Pea gravel: These are small, round, and smooth stones dredged from rivers. Often small, ⅜-inch (1 cm) crushed quarry stone is also called pea gravel.

Plumb: This means that a wall is exactly vertical.

Quarried stone: This is stone that has been cut, broken, or blasted from bedrock. Large blanks, weighing up to 15 tons (13.5 t) are then split, sawed, and broken into building, paving, and dimensional cut stone.

Quoin stone: This is a dimensionally cut cornerstone used for wall ends and window and door openings.

River rocks: These are rocks that have been rounded by the relentless force of water.

River slicks: These are small, mostly flat stones with rounded edges and smooth surfaces.

Rock: A rock is any naturally formed solid material made of the Earth's crust or petrified matter.

Rock dust: This is the screening from washed and sieved crushed stone, such as pea gravel (also called quarry screening).

Road bond (ABC or crusher run): This is a mixture of crushed stone, ⅜ to 1½ inches (1 to 3.8 cm) in size, and rock dust, which binds the mix together. Commonly used to build dirt roads or as a base for paved roads, road bond compacts well and is good for building up low spots in paving projects.

Rubble stones: These are irregularly shaped stones without obvious faces. Rubble stones are best used as backfill behind retaining walls and rough mortared stonework.

Running joint: A running joint occurs when the joints in a series of courses fall along the same vertical line, creating a weak spot in the stonework.

Sedimentary stone: This stone is created by the settling of layer upon layer of sediments deposited at the bottom of a body of water, such as an ocean or lake. The layers, referred to as strata, vary from a fraction of an inch to 10 feet (3 m) in thickness, with pressure and heat forming the stone. Limestone and sandstone are both sedimentary.

Shim stones: These are small, thin, and relatively flat pieces of stone that are used to adjust the overall height of larger stones.

The through or tie stone is the long stone extending well beyond the other wall stones. It helps to tie together the stonework and the packed crushed stone.

Stone: Rock that has been shaped by natural forces or by human persuasion, including natural weathered stone, river stone, building stone, millstones, and cobblestones.

Stretchers: These stones have long, horizontal faces and are usually used to lay on top of smaller stones in the course beneath them in order to break several joints with one stone.

Talus (Scree): This is a mass of broken stones and boulders that accumulates at the base of a cliff or mountain slope.

Through or tie stones: These stones will have a length equal to or slightly longer than the width of a freestanding wall. They are laid across the width of a wall at regular intervals every 3 feet (0.9 m), midway in the wall's height in order to provide extra structural integrity.

Wedges: These are small tapered bits of stone used to level larger stones, either from front to back or side to side. Whenever you trim stones, save the broken-off pieces, especially tapered ones, to serve as wedges.

There are, of course, other terms you'll become familiar with as you experience the many techniques and projects in this book.

The Search for Stone

For many artists and masons, finding the right material for a particular project is as satisfying as viewing the completed work. It's a great feeling when the stone you have searched for and selected complements and enhances your project.

A great deal has happened in the stone supply industry over the past 20 years. Every year, the number of stone suppliers has increased, making material more widely available. For years, stone yards were used to dealing primarily with stonemasons, building contractors, landscape architects, and landscaping professionals. These days, more and more homeowners are choosing to become involved in building their homes and creating their own landscapes. In response to this trend, many yards are making their businesses more visually appealing and finding more sophisticated and attractive ways of presenting stone to the general public.

Competition in the stone market has also created one-stop shopping centers for a wide variety of building stone, ornamental stone, pea stone, pavers, stone sculpture, Asian garden features, tools, and more. I visited one stone yard in Seattle, Washington, that left my head spinning after wandering through acres of stone. With this in mind, be prepared to make at least a couple of trips to the local stone yard before making any final decisions on your building materials and tools. If you have more than one stone supplier in your area, compare prices and quality. Sometimes stone yards and landscape suppliers will have brochures describing their stone and their masonry/landscape services; many have websites.

A good stone yard will offer a variety of stone.

Dimensional Stone

Some stone suppliers have the ability to custom cut and shape stone. Extremely large blocks of stone are first reduced to smaller cubes using feather wedges and hammers. Then, large wet saws and stone guillotines are used to create more specific shapes. This type of work is common for producing dimensional building stone, such as blocks of stone for carving and custom pavers.

Purchasing Stone

Stone is sold by weight. Often you'll find stone stacked on a pallet and enclosed in wire baskets or wrapped with plastic with a tag stating the weight. These pallets of hand-selected stone are usually sold as a unit. There have been times when I've only needed half a basket's worth to complete a job and was allowed to pick off the top half. Be sure to ask first before removing any stones from baskets.

Stone yards that deal in high volumes of stone may have a drive-on scale. In this situation, you drive your vehicle onto the scale before your stone is loaded to get your vehicle's empty weight. With the vehicle loaded, a second weight will tell how much stone you're buying. Another common method for weighing stone is a scale on which the pallets of stone are individually placed. For this, the stone yard will have a forklift to move the pallets around.

Handpicking Stone

Sometimes it's worth the effort to handpick your stone from bulk piles. I recommend handpicking particular pieces of stone, such as cornerstones and capstones for walls, treadstones for steps, specialty stones for water features, and landscaping boulders. Handpicking will take extra time, but once you know what to look for,

Stone is available in a wide variety of textures and colors.

Large blocks of sandstone weighing 10 to 15 tons (9 to 13.5 t) are split and sawed into pieces of flagstone.

it'll be time well spent. If you need more than a couple of tons of stone, you may want to buy some already on pallets and handpick the more specific stones. If the pile of bulk stone you want to pick through is small or looks picked over, ask when they'll be getting another load and come back then.

There's no guarantee that a stone yard or landscape supplier will have the stone you want when you want it. Plan in advance, and when you find what you're looking for, be prepared to purchase it then. The stone yard may be willing to hold the stone for a week or two if you're not ready for its delivery, providing the yard has the space.

If you're choosing landscape stones that are heavier than you can pick up, you may need to bring a friend along or ask for assistance from someone working at the yard. Most stone yards will have a forklift or front loader and an operator available. To identify and hold large landscape boulders, you'll need to mark them with surveyor's tape or a small spot of bright removable paint. (I go for the neon colors.) The paint can be removed with a wire brush.

If a stone yard has bulk piles of stone to choose from, most likely they'll charge you a nominal handpicking fee over the price per ton. One stone yard I go to has a "select" pile of stone that has a premium price. When this particular sandstone is gathered, it's graded as the truck is filled. I will spend less time picking through this pile, though I'll spend more money on the stone. The difference in the choices between the same stone in a random pile and the select one is considerable. Often I will pick through both piles.

Other Sources of Stone

If you live in a rocky area, there may be private and public lands you can visit in order to pick stone or boulders for free or a small fee. I don't advise picking stone off of someone's property without getting the owner's permission first.

A talus slope in British Columbia, Canada.

Although partially obscured by mosses and ferns, the walls of this abandoned quarry offer a glimpse of the local geology.

If you've found some stone, and it's not obvious who the owner is, do a little investigating. Ask people on the neighboring property, or if you can locate the property on a map, the local deed office can find the owner from tax records. If you live in a fairly rural setting, stone should be easy to find simply by asking around. There may be an active quarry in the area or old stone farm walls someone is eager to get rid of.

Quarry Sites

Abandoned quarry sites are excellent locations to find building stone, carving stones (limestone quarries), landscape boulders, and standing stones. If the quarry is completely abandoned, you'll have to locate the current owner and ask if they're willing to open the quarry for you.

Scree and Talus

Scree and talus are terms that describe rocks of all sizes that accumulate at the base of a rocky slope. Usually there's a bold rock face at the top of the slope with an area clear of trees and vegetation below where the stones gather. The physical geography of this type of setting is easy to locate by sight, and if it's easy to get a truck there, you may be able to gather an excellent selection of stone. Extreme caution should be used when walking across these slopes. The stones are loose and still subject to movement. The safest place to pick is toward the bottom of the slope.

House Sites

Old house sites can also provide good stone, but be cautious of stone that has been through a fire. The intense heat may have weakened the stone. You may come across an old mortared stone foundation that will require a pry bar or a digging bar to loosen the stones. A scaling hammer is used specifically to remove old mortar from brick and stone. A brick mason's hammer will also work.

The Perfect Stone

There is such a thing as the perfect building stone. I describe it as one that I don't have to move more than once or twice before it's set in a wall. When searching for stone for a project, you'll most likely want to use the stone already available at the local stone yard, unless you have an unlimited budget. Avoid stones that are soft and crumble at their edges; they won't weather well or hold up under the weight of other stones.

Most stone is chosen with consideration for its color, texture, strength, and price. A stone's workability is also something to consider, particularly if you're new to stonework. When selecting stone for a particular project, you need to consider the availability of a good selection of shapes and sizes. Even with a good selection of stone, it's likely you'll have to shape some of the stones by breaking and trimming to fit them properly into a wall or paving project.

Once you've worked with stone, it will forever change the way you look at it. Physically handling a stone gives you an immediate appreciation of its weight and density. Each stone is unique, which is what makes working with stone both challenging and interesting. Breaking a stone in two across its grain or splitting it into thinner layers along its grain reveals more information about the stone's structure. When you have moved, sorted, split, broken, shaped, moved again, and finally stacked a ton of stone, you'll begin to know that particular type of stone, appreciate its qualities, and anticipate its limitations.

CHAPTER TWO

TOOLS AND BASIC TECHNIQUES

Stones mark the beginning of primitive tool technology. Strike two stones together and eventually one stone will break against the other, leaving fragments with sharp edges. These sharp edged flakes were used to collect and process food and work other materials such as wood or animal hides. The earliest hammers were simply stones weighing 2 to 3 pounds (0.9 to 1.4 kg) gripped against the palm of the hand. The point here is not to impart knowledge of primitive tools, but to remember the simple beauty of this ancient material we're using. When you think about it, a steel hammerhead with a wooden handle is still a simple tool.

Getting Started

Most of the tools you'll need for the projects in this book are simple, fairly inexpensive, and easy to maintain. Hardware stores and home improvement centers carry everything you need, and I've found many of my tools at flea markets, antique stores, and yard sales. The stone-working techniques detailed here are also simple and designed to get the job done safely and effectively.

More specific tools will be listed as they're needed for each project, and tools and techniques for lifting boulders appear on page 25.

Lifting, Hauling, and Carrying Stone

Whether you're working with gravel or boulders, you need a safe and effective way to get your stones to your work site.

Wheelbarrows

A stout, metal wheelbarrow is a must for moving stones. The standard barrow (or pan) sizes are 4 and 6 cubic feet (0.12 and 0.18 m³). I prefer the larger model, which can also be used for mixing mortar. The plastic barrows will work; however, they don't hold up to a lot of abuse. Two-wheeled wooden garden carts are capable of handling light loads, though the wheel rims and axles on these carts can't withstand heavy loads. A wooden brick barrow has the identical frame and single wheel of a wheelbarrow, but its barrow is made of wooden slats and designed more like a cart. The wooden slats cover the bottom, with three of the sides left open, making it easier to load and unload bags of mortar and loads of stone. No matter what type of barrow you choose, it should have a large pneumatic tire, which will give you more control over uneven ground.

The brickbarrow is a sturdy and lightweight cousin of the standard wheelbarrow and is ideal for moving stones and bags of cement.

Using a Wheelbarrow

To move very large stones, first turn the wheelbarrow on edge, right next to the stone. Push the stone into the barrow. Then lift the stone up onto its end and move around to the other side of the wheelbarrow. Pull the wheelbarrow and stone toward you until the wheelbarrow is upright.

For moving heavy loads up an incline, have a second person in front grabbing the lip of the barrow while pulling upward and forward at the same time. If there's only one person, zigzag up a slope when possible or take lighter loads. Having the correct tire pressure is crucial for these maneuvers.

Hand Trucks and Ball Carts

A small hand truck with pneumatic tires is easy to handle and capable of hauling 200 to 300 pounds (91 to 136 kg). If your work site if fairly level, you can load large, blocky stones, capstones, or small boulders on a hand truck and move them wherever they're needed.

Centering heavy materials directly over a wheelbarrow's tire lightens the load on the handles.

Moving larger pieces of stone often requires larger equipment. Though still manually operated, a ball cart is capable of moving these 250-pound (113.5 kg) slabs of flagstone.

Ball carts have a larger metal frame and bigger tires than the hand truck. They're designed to move trees and shrubs with bulky root balls. I've found them to be extremely helpful when moving large slabs of stone weighing 200 to 300 pounds (91 to 136 kg) each. Your local nursery or tree farm may have a ball cart they'd be willing to lend or rent, or they could direct you to a source for purchasing one.

Using a Hand Truck or Ball Cart

To use either the hand truck or ball cart, position it as close as possible to the stone you're going to move. With its frame or lip along the bottom front edge at ground level, slide the edge underneath the stone. Center the stone on the cart and tilt the truck back slightly toward you. Then either push or pull it in the direction you want to go.

A stack of building stone can be moved about easily with a small hand truck.

Heavy-duty come-alongs, one with chains and one with cable.

A "Come-Along"

The "come-along"—a small, portable, hand-operated winch—helps move very large stones. The model I use has a cable drum and is rated to pull 1½ tons (1525 kg), which is plenty of pulling power. Heavier-duty models, made to pull or lift 3 to 5 tons (3051 to 5085 kg), are also available. These larger models incorporate chains or heavy-duty cables. When using come-alongs, keep an assortment of chains, webbing straps, and ropes on hand.

Buckets

Five-gallon (19 L) buckets can often be found on construction sites, at bakeries, and for sale at home improvement centers. They're invaluable for hauling gravel, sand, water, and for collecting smaller stones. I store my hammers and chisels in them, and I turn empty buckets upside down when I need a seat.

Ramps

Pieces of lumber, 4 to 8 feet (1.2 to 2.4 m) long, make good ramps when you need to move large stones into a truck bed or when setting large capstones on a retaining wall.

Using a Ramp

For moving large building stones or capstones from ground level up onto a wall, set one end of the ramp on the wall. Slide the stone onto the board and stand it up on its edge. Then, walk it up the ramp or flip it end over end up the ramp. Two people working together can slide a stone up the inclined board.

A four-foot-long (1.2 m) ramp using a 4 x 4 piece of lumber.

Log Rollers

Also keep a few 3-foot-long (0.9 m) round logs, 4 to 10 inches (10.2 to 25.4 cm) in diameter, on hand to serve as wheels for rolling large flat stones from one place to another.

You can also use lumber as "tracks" for your rollers.

Using Log Rollers

You'll need four log ends that are perfectly round for moving large slabs. If the stone has at least one flat side, it can be moved with just log rollers. For irregular-shaped stones, build a simple stone boat made with 4 × 4-inch (10.2 × 10.2-cm) timbers as runners connected with a 2 × 5-foot (0.6 × 1.5-m) plywood deck.

Moving a stone using long rollers is much easier and more fun with at least two people. Set the stone boat on the ground alongside the stone you're moving, pointed in the direction you want to move the stone. To set the stone on the boat, use two digging bars and blocks of wood as levers and fulcrums. As you lift the stone, chuck blocks of wood underneath. Lift the stone up to the height of the boat, then slide it onto the plywood deck.

Using the levers and fulcrum, pry up on the front of the runners high enough to slip a log roller underneath. Push from the opposite end using the pry bar, if needed, rolling it a couple of feet, then setting another log roller at the front of the boat. Keep positioning the rollers at the front and pushing the boat along, gathering rollers from the rear to be set in the front as needed.

Pry Bar

A pry bar tied to a stone and used as a lever reduces the force required to move a stone.

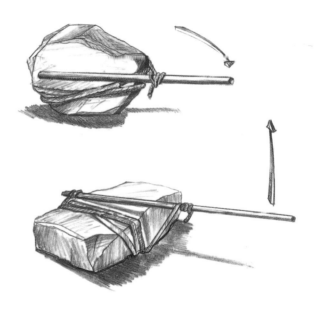

Lifting Stones by Yourself

Building stones are moved a minimum of three times: when they're gathered and delivered, when they're sorted out at the project site, and finally, when they're set in the project. The effect on the body of picking up one stone after another is cumulative and really only something to worry about if you're choosing this as a career.

Start a project slowly, stretch out before and after working, and consider the following tips:

- The proper way to lift a stone is by crouching down with your knees bent and back straight. Pick up the stone and stand up, using your leg muscles to lift while holding the stone close to your body. Use this method with particularly heavy stones, and avoid twisting the upper body while you're lifting. Bending over to pick up smaller stones is fine; just be mindful of what you're doing.

- When crouched down about to lift a heavy stone, first take a couple of deep breaths and focus your attention on your body lifting the stone.

- For walking with a heavy stone, hold it close to you, resting it on an upper thigh if you need to.

- When two or more people are lifting a large stone, first agree on which direction you're going and take slow steady steps together.

Pounding and Breaking Stone

No matter how many times you read about breaking stone, you won't know how to break stone until you do it, and do it, and do it. After a lot of practice, you'll learn just where to grip the handle of your hammer in relationship to the power your arm is delivering with its swing. As your hand-to-eye coordination improves, you'll notice the stones breaking where you want them to more often. Using a banker is helpful when you're first starting out. A stone banker is anything that helps absorb the shock of a hammer blow when you're working on a stone. A stone banker will improve your ability to trim and break stones more accurately and consistently. You can create a simple banker by dumping two 5-gallon (19 l) buckets of sand or pea gravel on the ground close to where you're working.

Hammers

There are a number of hammers in the 1- to 4-pound (0.45 to 1.8-kg) range that stonemasons use to break and split stone, including brick-and-block mason's hammers, stonemason's hammers, mash hammers, and blacksmith's forging hammers. Of the dozen or so hammers that I currently own, my favorites are a 2½-pound (1.1 kg) *blacksmith's forging hammer* and a 3-pound (1.4 kg)

Stonemason's hammers.

stonemason's hammer (also referred to as a *spalling hammer*). You can use both of these hammers to break away large sections of unwanted stone.

The *mash hammer* comes in 2-, 3-, and 4-pound (0.9, 1.4, and 1.8 kg) weights and is my hammer of choice when using chisels to split a stone with the grain or to score a stone for breaking across the grain. A 4-pound (1.8 kg) *bush hammer*, with a deep-grooved waffle head, is handy for evening out the high spots on the surfaces of softer stones, such as sandstone. A 3-pound (1.4 kg) *rubber or leather mallet* is useful for setting mortared flagstone and other paving materials. The lighter hammers such as the *brick-and-block mason's hammers* work well for trimming smaller stones and thinner sections of stone. *Sledgehammers* are the heavy hitters, weighing 4 to 16 pounds (1.8 to 7.3 kg). They're generally used to make smaller stones out of big ones. My 5- and 12-pound (2.3 and 5.4 kg) sledges see the most use; occasionally I'll use my 16-pound (7.3 kg) hammer to break extremely thick or dense stones, such as granite.

The waffle-head of a bush hammer can also be used to leave a highly textured surface on carved limestone.

Brick-and-block mason's hammers.

Shaping and Splitting Stone

Successfully shaping and/or splitting a stone without shattering it is that mysterious part of stone work that most people find so fascinating. Stone responds to the striking of a hammer according to its density and structural makeup. I do most of my stone shaping by gripping the stone with my right hand and bracing it against my right thigh (I'm left-handed). Remember to always wear safety glasses when using hammers and chisels.

To trim a tapered edge or remove a section of stone, turn the stone's edge you're working on slightly out and away from you. Strike the outside edge of the stone with the squared end of the hammerhead. Thin the stone's thickness first from this angle, then flip it over and continue thinning the stone so it has a tapered edge. Strike the thinned edge back to square up its edge, showing the thickness of the stone again. Repeat if more of the stone needs to be removed.

Some stones will have one or more natural fissures or clefts along their bedding seams. To split a small stone along its seam with a hammer, stand the stone up on edge so the seam is facing up. Then, using the tapered end of a stonemason's hammer, strike along the seam until it opens up and the stone splits. To split a stone with a large surface area, such as a capstone or flagstone, read the section on using chisels (page 28).

Sledgehammers weighing 16, 12, and 5 pounds (7.3, 5.4, and 2.3 kg), respectively.

A 2.5-pound blacksmith's hammer was used to break away the tapered edge of a piece of flagging.

Striking this stone several times along a visible seam caused the stone to crack and then neatly separate into two pieces.

The deep-grooved waffle head of a bush hammer acts like a grid of small-pointed chisels. When the waffle head strikes a high spot on a stone's surface, it breaks the surface up into smaller pieces. Repeated striking pulverizes the high spot, creating an even surface. This is a good way to round off the sharp edge on a stone, as well.

Making Smaller Stones

A general rule of thumb is that the larger the stone you want to break, the bigger the hammer you'll need. This is particularly true in relation to a stone's thickness. The weight of a sledgehammer's head and its long handle create a dynamic force when struck against stone. Sometimes you get the stone to break just the way you want it to, though often you'll end up with a bunch of smaller pieces that make good backfill in a retaining wall or core material for a freestanding wall.

For the best control of the hammer, crouch down in front of the stone, raise the hammer above your head, and strike the stone where you want it to break. For an even rift (break) of stones with a large surface area, strike at several points along the line you want to crack. A 5- to 10-pound (2.3 to 4.5-kg) sledgehammer will work for most situations. I once had to break large 6-inch-thick (15.2-cm) slabs of granite into squared corners for a couple of mortared-stone gateposts. A 20-pound (9-kg) sledge was required in that situation.

Cutting, Scoring, Splitting, and Chipping Stone

Chisels are used for scoring, splitting, cutting, and chipping stone. Although a hammer will work alone to split or break stone, in some situations, using the correct chisel gives you more control.

Chisels

The least expensive chisels for stonework are *cold chisels*, 8 to 10 inches (20 to 25 cm) long, with shafts about ¾ inch (2 cm) in diameter and blades ranging from 1 to 2 inches wide (2.5 to 5.1 cm). (Note the end of the

A 12-pound (5.4 kg) sledgehammer splitting a piece of dense sandstone.

Stonemason Jeff Thue using a sledgehammer to split a boulder.

From left to right: a hand-point chisel, a hand-set chisel, and a hand-tracer chisel.

blade of a cold chisel will be beveled on both sides of the cutting edge.) Also in this category is a *brick chisel*, with a wider blade of 3 inches (7.6 cm).

The chisels used by professional stonemasons are heavier, will last longer, and are three to four times more expensive than the standard cold chisels. Made of alloy steel, these professional tools are also available with carbide tips that hold an edge 20 times longer than regular steel.

The three basic chisels used by professional stonemasons are the *hand point*, the *hand tracer*, and the *hand sets*. These chisels are available through masonry supply businesses and some home hardware stores.

Using Chisels

Hand point chisels are used to chisel away high spots on a stone. They're also useful for tracing lines and chipping off edges on a stone. A hand set has a blunt, squared edge that's good for breaking away unwanted sections of stone. Hand tracers are used to score straight lines on stones and split stone. Many types of stone

(sedimentary, in particular) have visible bedding seams that can be split, making thinner pieces of stone.

To split a stone with a hammer and hand tracer, stand the stone up on edge, and set it either on the ground or on a banker (see page 26). Place the chisel's

Jimmy wedges.

From left to right: a brick chisel and three cold chisels.

cutting edge along the seam you want to split. Tap the chisel with a 2- to 3-pound (0.9 to 1.4-kg) hammer, moving the chisel along the seam from one end to the next, repeating the chiseling along the seam until it starts to open. Turn the stone until the opposite end is up, and chisel along the same seam. As it starts to open, the ringing of the stone and chisel will turn to a dull thud. At that point, the stone should split into two pieces. For large stones, start the cleft with the chisel, working it along the length of the seam, until you get an opening. Then use a few jimmy wedges set out along the seam, with the tapered ends placed in the cleft. Tap each wedge evenly into the seam until the stone splits.

The hand point chisel directs the force from a hammer into its single point. To lift high spots from a stone's surface, chisel with the point around the section you're removing. Chisel into the center of a high spot, changing the angle of the chisel as it breaks up. Continue chiseling from the edges and into the center, and then use a cold chisel or tracer to even the surface out.

Hand sets, with their blunt, squared cutting edges, are useful for breaking away large sections along the edge of a stone. I use one exclusively for shaping 2-inch-thick (5.1-cm) sandstone pavers. While kneeling on the paver, move the chisel along the outside edge, chipping away small sections of stone with each strike from a hammer. Angle the striking end of the chisel toward you, putting the cutting edge in the opposite direction, which is where you want the stone chips to fly.

Saws

A double-insulated electrical circular saw rated at 13 amps or more, with a 7 1/4-inch-diameter (18.4-cm) abrasive or diamond blade, is useful for scoring flagstone before you break it. Both abrasive and diamond blades work well on medium and soft stone.

A masonry cut-off saw, with an abrasive or diamond blade 12 to 14 inches (30 to 36 cm) in diameter will cut stone, concrete, or metal. These saws are similar to chainsaws, but they make use of a large disklike blade instead of a chain. They weigh around 40 pounds (18.2 kg), so they're not for everyone! Check them out at your local equipment rental center.

Using Saws

Cutting stone to mark a line to be rifted (broken) or even cutting all the way through works only on medium and soft stones, such as sandstone and limestone.

The stone I cut most often with a saw is a medium-density sandstone used in mortared and dry-laid paving. First define the portion to be removed by using a straightedge and chisel to score a line across the stone's surface. Prop the stone up at a 15-degree angle, with the marked end at the lower end. Position a hose with a nozzle at the top of the stone so that you can direct a slow, steady stream of water down the stone and across the scored line. Put on your safety glasses and earplugs.

Next, using a double-insulated circular saw with an abrasive or diamond blade, cut a straight, shallow groove, ¼ inch (6 mm) deep, along the scored line. Position the front edge of the saw's baseplate on top of the stone, with the saw's guide mark over the scored line. Hold the saw at an angle so the blade doesn't touch the stone. Turn the saw on, carefully lower the spinning blade down until it touches the start of the scored line, and guide the saw gently back and forth. Don't exert any downward pressure on the blade; instead, allow the weight of the saw to do the cutting. Lifting the blade guard makes it easier to control the action of the blade. Do this with extreme care! The water flowing over the stone will reduce dust in the air as well as wear on the blade.

Two important warnings: Make absolutely sure that your circular saw is double-insulated before you run water anywhere near it. Also, if you're plugged into an extension cord, waterproof the joint where the cord and the saw plug join by wrapping it tightly with duct tape.

Not for the timid, a masonry cut-off saw is an aggressive tool capable of cutting through medium-density stone, concrete, or metal.

A steady stream of water directed at the saw's blade reduces wear and rock dust. Have a second person direct the nozzle while you saw.

The setup for using a masonry cut-off saw is similar to using a circular saw. This saw has more power, more weight, and a larger blade. It helps to have a second person holding the nozzle and directing a stream of water directly on the blade. When you're cutting, allow the spinning blade to lightly touch down on the stone.

Trimming Stones for Walls
by Robbie Oates, professional mason

Imagine that one long edge of your worktable represents the face of your wall and that the surface of the table represents a course of stone in the wall. Select a "blank" (the stone you'd like to trim) and position it on the table as if you were setting it into the wall.

Next, pull the blank out slightly so that its face overlaps the long edge of the table. Now imagine a vertical plane rising from the table edge and slicing through the overlapping stone. Your goal is to trim the stone so that the four edges around its face all rest on this plane.

▶ Using your square as a straightedge and a 3-inch-wide (8-cm) chisel as a marker, trace a line across the top of the stone. This line should rest right over the edge of the tabletop.

▲ Now mark the ends of the stone in the same fashion, placing one edge of the square on the tabletop and aligning the other edge with the edge of the table. Also mark the bottom of the stone.

◀ Step back to check the traced lines. They should all align with the imaginary plane rising from the long edge of the table.

◀ The next step is to create a preliminary fracture in the rock's crystalline structure. You won't actually break the rock at this stage, but the fracture will make the rock much easier to trim when you're ready. Position a 3-inch-wide (8-cm) chisel on the traced line and strike it, using moderate force, with a hammer. Repeat, moving the chisel along the lines on all four sides of the rock.

▲ I use a carbide-tipped chisel to deepen the fracture, working my way around the lines once again.

▲ Next comes trimming. Working your way around the lines, strike the chisel much harder than you did to create the fracture. Your goal is to remove shards of rock along the traced lines. Work along the top and bottom surfaces first.

▲ To trim each end, position the rock with the end facing up. To keep the rock stable, be sure to prop it up firmly with other rocks.

▲ Finally, trim away any ragged edges.

▲ With a bit of practice, you'll soon be able to turn out a well-trimmed face.

◄ If you'd like to make a cornerstone to place at the end of the wall, repeat these steps to trim one end of the stone. Position your square as shown at left so that your traced lines (and the face you're about to trim) will be perpendicular to the face you've already trimmed.

▶ The stone shown underneath the chisels is a fully trimmed cornerstone.

Putting It All Together

When laying tight stonework, be it mortared or dry-laid, developing a critical eye is as important as having a good selection of stone to choose from. Once a stone is set in a wall, you don't want to have to take it back out. If there are any large protrusions that will keep the next course from being laid properly, it's best to remove them before you move on to the next stone. If you're frustrated by the choices of stone and find you're unhappy with what's laid, you may need to take some of the work out. Sloppy work looks bad by itself—when mixed with good work it looks really bad.

If you can't find a stone to fit in a particular spot, you'll have to make one fit. Start with something at least close to the shape you want. In stone-wall building, the majority of the work I do to shape a stone is done with a hammer alone. Using a hammer to break and trim stone takes a certain amount of concentration and coordination. It's not difficult, but there's more to it than just swinging a hammer at a stone. Focus on where you want the hammer to hit, the angle of the hammer's head while it's swinging, and the amount of force in each swing. Fewer, more decisive strikes from hammer to stone are better than several taps. Each time you strike against a stone it sends vibrations through its structure, causing the stone to weaken. For example, if the stone is sedimentary, constant tapping may cause it to split between layers into thinner pieces.

With practice, the hammers and chisels will begin to feel more comfortable in your hands. If you need more control while working with a hammer, simply choke up on the handle. Choking up means gripping the hammer's handle closer to the hammer's head. By gripping toward the end of the hammer's handle, you'll increase the force behind each swing, but have less control.

Squared and round-point shovels.

Fresh Cuts

Any time you break a stone in two or remove a small section, it'll leave the markings of a fresh cut. Fresh cuts are most visible on weathered fieldstone and less obvious on quarried stone. Fresh cuts will take years to blend in, so keep them to a minimum, or choose to spread them out evenly throughout the stonework. Some cuts are left with sharp edges. By rounding these edges off a bit, the cut will be less obvious. Strike these sharp edges with a hammer's squared face to round them over.

Other Tools

Two types of shovels come in handy for grading sites and shoveling sand and gravel: one has a square blade, the other a round blade. A shovel with a square blade is most efficient for leveling rough spots of soil and shoveling sand and gravel. A shovel with a round blade works for general digging. I use shovels with short handles when I'm digging in tight spots and at odd angles.

Mattocks

Pry bar

Tamper

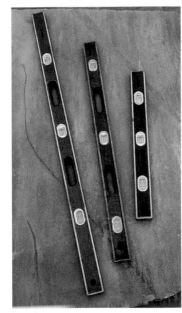

Levels

The *mattock* is similar to a miner's pickaxe, but instead of having two opposing picks, it may have either a pick or wedge-shaped blade at one end of the metal head and a slightly curved digging blade at the opposite end. This tool is useful for loosening packed earth and embedded rocks from the ground.

A *pry bar*, also referred to as a shale bar or digging bar, is a solid piece of steel, 1 to 1½ inches (2.5 to 3.8 cm) thick that's tapered at one end and beveled or wedge-shaped at the other end. It's most useful for adjusting the positions of large stones and for prying stones out of the ground. Any pry bar that doesn't bend easily is a good one. These bars vary in length from 4 to 6 feet (1.2 to 1.8 m) and weigh around 30 pounds (13.6 kg). You can locate one at your local hardware store or home improvement center.

Crowbars, which are similar to pry bars, but smaller and lighter, make effective stone-prying tools. They range from 2 to 3 feet (0.6 to 0.9 m) in length. One end

of the tool is flat and slightly flared; the other end is curved in a "J" shape.

You'll need a *tamper* to compact soil or gravel for dry-laid projects. This tool is simply a flat piece of metal attached to a long handle.

A *measuring tape* is necessary to have on site. For general use, I prefer a 16- or 25-foot (4.8 or 7.5 m) tape. Longer ones are bulkier and heavier. The wider, heavy gauge tapes will last much longer than the narrow, flimsy ones.

You'll need at least one level for setting steps, pavers, and benches. The highest quality *levels* are made of wood and metal; less expensive ones are made of plastic. A 2-foot (61-cm) level is handy for setting step treads and adjusting individual stones within a paving project. For gauging the level and pitch of several stones in a paving project, a 4- or 6- foot (1.2- or 1.8-m) level works best.

With consistent use, the edges of hammers will round off, the cutting edges of chisels will blunt, and digging implements will dull. So, regular sharpening is a must. I use an electric bench grinder and a ⅓-horsepower motor and a 6-inch (15.2-cm) grinding wheel. You can also use a belt sander and/or manually sharpen your tools with a vise and metal file. If you don't want to buy a grinder, take your tools to a professional sharpening service. Be aware that the cutting edge of a chisel does not need to be sharp like a knife's blade.

Safety Equipment

There's no way to predict which way rock chips will fly when breaking and trimming stone. For this reason, safety glasses are a must when working with stone. I discovered a lightweight pair of safety glasses that offer full protection by wrapping around the sides of my head, while still providing good ventilation. When I'm working, I keep these glasses dangling from a strap around my neck, ready to be worn at any time.

Wearing tough leather gloves while working with stone is the best way to protect your hands. Make sure they fit well; loose gloves won't let you get a good grip on stones or tools. For good support and protection, wear leather boots. When you're working on paving projects, knee pads or garden pads will save wear and tear on your trousers and knees.

Most stonework involves a lot of bending down and lifting. This requires a fair amount of stamina. I suggest starting off with a simple, small-scale project and working into it, slowly. I've avoided serious injury over the past 15 years as a stonemason, but there certainly have been a number of scrapes, bruises, and pinched fingers along the way, most of which happened when I wasn't paying attention.

Before You Begin

Many of the projects in this book are for those with beginning and intermediate levels of stoneworking skills, and a few of the projects will be a bit more challenging. With any given stone project, the building situation is going to be different because of details specific to a site, the materials used, and the level of knowledge and experience of the builder.

Sometimes a large landscape project can be broken down into smaller ones, allowing months, even years, to complete the total picture. If you are a do-it-yourselfer, then you may already have experience with this and know how realistic your goals are. Having an overall picture of what you want in your landscape is the first step, while leaving room for change to new ideas. Taking on projects yourself can be exciting, and any of these projects can be a personally rewarding experience that you can share with your family and friends.

It's a grand feeling to conceptualize a stone feature in the landscape, gather the materials, build it, and complete the project, all because you think you can. That's why I generally encourage people to start out with a small project that's doable; positive results are wonderful. Sometimes you may feel some techniques are, quite simply, over your head. Don't let that discourage you. Call on the opinion and/or services of a professional, or seek out information in books. Other times, you may feel just comfortable enough moving forward with the technique and seeing what develops. Go with your instincts, but also don't hesitate to stop and seek assistance when needed.

CHAPTER THREE

DRY-STACKED WALLS

In this section, you'll learn about methods of building that have been used and improved upon since ancient times. For wall building, these methods include selecting good stone, fitting stones tightly, and relying on the forces of gravity and friction to keep your project together.

A dry-laid freestanding farm wall in Saunders Town, Rhode Island

Part of the beauty of dry-stone walls and other dry-laid projects is that you don't need elaborate footings of concrete and steel as you do with most mortared stone walls. The type of building I'll detail in this chapter allows minor amounts of settling without undermining the project's integrity. Shifting of any sort in a mortared project will cause the mortar between the stones to crack and eventually break away. When this happens, moisture seeps into the stonework, causing further damage.

There are basically two different types of dry-stone walls. One is a freestanding wall and the other is a retaining-style wall. A freestanding wall can be built almost anywhere on top of stable soil. Freestanding walls are double sided, having two faces that are tied together using bond and through stones. Retaining walls, on the other hand, have a single face and are built with a slight lean into a bank of soil. You'll find this style of wall building in mountainous and hilly areas, or anywhere there's a bank of soil that needs to be contained.

The craft of building dry-stacked freestanding walls has been practiced around the world, and nowhere is this more evident than in the British Isles and Ireland. The agricultural communities of these areas are synonymous with stone-wall building, with many walls dating back to the eighteenth century and others to prehistory. In the U.S., a proud heritage of wall building is evident in the webwork of thousands of miles of dry stonewalls that in many regions define the landscape.

Immigrants from Ireland and the British Isles brought their wall-building skills to America. In the Colonies of New England, stone was so plentiful it was considered a nuisance, and clearing stones from the land was a constant chore. It made sense to neatly stack the stones into walls that took up less space. They also proved useful as boundary markers and fences for livestock.

A freestanding single-stone fence in Southern India

Building a Freestanding Wall

The wall detailed here is 4 feet (1.2 m) high, 2 feet (0.6 m) thick at its base, and 24 feet (7.2 m) long. Of course, yours can be any size you desire.

Considerations

Freestanding walls can be anywhere from 3 to 6 feet (0.9 to 1.8 m) tall. They make great privacy walls and garden borders and look wonderful in a landscape. With their double facing and stout stone footings, freestanding walls are a bit more involved than retaining walls of the same height and will take more time to build. So, when starting out, don't overcommit yourself to a project you don't have the time to complete. Try a short length of double-stone walling before tackling a larger project.

A dry-laid freestanding wall relies on its batter, gravity, a tight fitting of stones, a thoroughly packed center (core), and through and bond stones to bind the two faces of the wall together. Water that manages to enter the wall (properly set capstones prevent most water from entering in the first place) exits easily. A well-built wall will last at least a couple hundred years, needing only minimum maintenance.

Selecting Stone

When selecting stone for your wall, choose relatively flat stones that are 4 to 24 inches (10.2 to 61 cm) wide and 2 to 6 inches (5.1 to 15.2 cm) thick. There are also some specific sizes and shapes of stone you'll need to be aware of when you go to gather your wall-building material:

- Your foundation stones will be the largest and heaviest stones. They should be fairly flat and similar in thickness.
- Bond stones, reaching across about two-thirds of the wall's thickness, further bind the two faces of a wall in the wall's interior. These stones will be set as often as possible with at least one every 4 feet (1.2 m) from one side to the next as the courses of stone are being stacked.
- Your through stones need to span the complete width of the wall. These stones are placed every few feet along the course that is midway in the wall's height. Through stones that extend several inches beyond the wall's face on each side of the wall provide maximum strength.

Volunteers from the Dry Stone Conservancy in Lexington, Kentucky, admiring their handiwork

- Capstones, also referred to as the "cover course," are laid horizontally along the top of a wall, binding the upper course of face stones together. One way to finish the wall is by laying single capstones that span the width of the wall. These stones will be around 16 inches (40.6 cm) wide, allowing for a 1-inch (2.5-cm) overhang on both sides, while butting up to each other as they're set.
- Traditionally, this type of wall is completed with a row of coping stones set on top of the capstones. Relatively thin coping stones are stood up vertically like books on a shelf or at an angle of 15 degrees. The two different styles of coping are single and double copes. For single cope stones, the ideal height is 10 to 12 inches (25.4 to 30.5 cm). Single copes should span the entire surface of the last leveled face course or the top of the capstones. Double cope stones are slightly smaller, standing 8 to 10 inches (20.3 to 25.4 cm) tall.

Figure 1 Trimming a stone for a better fit.

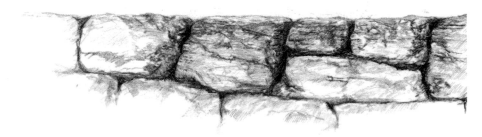

Figure 2 Two small stones can be used when a shorter stone is set between two larger ones.

How Much Stone You'll Need

With 1 ton (0.9 t) of stone, you can build a section of wall 3 feet (0.9 m) long, 2 feet (0.6 m) wide at the base, and 4 feet (1.2 m) tall. For a wall 12 feet (3.6 m) long, you'll need 4 tons (3.6 t) of stones that have relatively flat top and bottom surfaces, 4 to 24 inches (10.2 to 61 cm) wide and 2 to 6 inches (5.1 to 15.2 cm) thick.

Shaping Stones for Walls

This information is useful for any type of wall you build, dry laid or mortared (even veneered). Refer to Chapter 2 for details on how to use your tools to trim stone.

The main thing to remember when trimming stones for a wall is that a stone's fit isn't complete until each stone around it is also set. Ideally, the base and sides of each stone should be perpendicular to the stone's face. If the sides aren't squared up, you'll need to trim the stone as needed to fit with the surrounding stones. The top and bottom surfaces of a stone you're setting in a wall should be free of any protrusions that decrease its contact with surrounding stones and would cause it to wobble. An even surface will have better contact with the previous course and the following one. Most stones will need to be worked with a hammer and or shimmed with smaller stones to achieve a proper fit. It may take a minor tap with a hammer to square the thin edge of a stone, or you might have to dramatically alter the stone's shape by breaking away a large section (figure 1).

As you work, remember that the top portion of the stones you're setting will have to be dealt with when you're laying the next course. The heights of two adjacent stones need to match up where they meet, forming a vertical joint. If they don't, smaller stones can be used to make up the difference, or one of the stones may need to be trimmed (figure 2). Marking the portion of stone to be trimmed with a crayon is helpful when first learning to shape the stones with a hammer. Any stone trimming should be done off the wall, with the stone placed on a banker (see page 26).

When I'm wall building, I'll look for a stone that closely matches the shape of the next space to fill. I'll place the stone I've chosen on the wall with the most obvious face showing. If the fit doesn't feel right, I might flip the stone over or spin it around and show another face.

Height and Width Proportions

The freestanding wall described here has a *batter* (or lean) of 1:6, the universal standard. This means that for every 6 inches (15.2 cm) of height, the wall will taper in 1 inch (2.5 cm) for each side of the wall (that's 2 inches [5.1 cm] total). The height of this wall (4 feet [1.2 m]), minus the foundation, cover course, and coping stones is 3 feet (0.9 m). With 36 inches (0.9 m) of height, there are six 6-inch (15.2-cm) increments, meaning the wall will decrease 12 inches (30.5 cm) in thickness from the bottom to the top (figure 3). Walls with a consistent thickness throughout can and have been built; however, a wall with battered sides will last longer, has more character, and uses less stone.

Site Setup

This information will also be useful for any large project you undertake. An organized project site is more productive, more enjoyable to work in, and safer. Once your stones have been delivered, spend some time sorting them into piles of foundation stones, wall stones, and coping stones, dividing the material evenly along both sides of the wall's foundation area. Place the largest stones closest and along the length of the proposed wall. These will be used first in the foundation. The next largest pieces will be used for the courses of facing in the bottom half of the wall. Squared, blocky stones will be needed for wall heads or wall ends at both ends of the wall. Set long, rectangular stones around 30 inches (79.2 cm) long, in a separate pile to be used as through stones. Set capstones and thinner pieces for coping toward the back of the piles, because they'll be used last. Take this time to inventory your stones, and lay them out so you can see what you're working with before you start building.

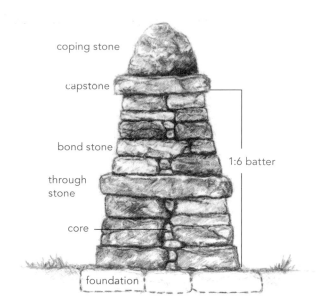

Figure 3 Profile of a freestanding wall

Keep a path about 4 feet (1.2 m) wide between the wall and the piles of stone. It's easy to scan the piles of stone if they're close at hand, but you don't want to stumble over them. As you work the stones to fit them in your wall, your work area will become littered with rock chips and discarded pieces of stone. Before you know it, there will hardly be any space in front of the wall to move around in. An occasional cleanup of the site will make for a more efficient and safer workspace. As you reorganize your work site, collect any rock chips that can work as shims, wedges, or filling for the core and place them in small piles along the wall's foundation.

Preparing the Foundation

A well-built, solid stone foundation is critical for the longevity of a freestanding stone wall. There are two ways of building the foundation: one with a perimeter that's even with the base of the wall, and the other with a perimeter that extends slightly beyond the wall's base.

A typical freestanding farm wall in New England, U.S.A. Such walls can average 6 feet (1.8 m) in width at the base.

A projection of 2 to 4 inches (5.1 to 10.2 cm) will increase the foundation's strength and the overall stability of the wall. Extending the foundation beyond the wall's base is recommended for walls 4 feet (1.2 m) tall and taller (see figure 3 on page 42).

To mark off the foundation, drive two stakes in the ground at one end of the wall, marking the width of the foundation (in this case, 34 inches [86.4 cm]—that's allowing 4 inches [10.2 cm] extra on each side). Measure 24 feet (7.2 m) along the length of the foundation and drive the other two stakes into the ground the same distance apart as the first two, leaving at least 6 inches (15.2 cm) of the stakes above ground.

Connect the stakes along the foundation's length with nylon string. Wrap the string around the stakes and pull it taut so that it's 3 to 5 inches (7.6 to 12.7 cm)

Figure 4 Foundation stones set to the height of string lines

above ground level. The area marked off should look like a long, narrow rectangle (figure 4). The general thickness of your foundation stones will determine the depth of the trench needed to set them in. When laid in the trench, the stones should be level with or slightly above the ground.

You need to lay the foundation on a firm, level, packed surface of soil. Remove any stones that project up through the soil and pack any holes with soil. Then compact any loose soil with a tamper. If you encounter rocks sunk in the ground that are too large to remove, clear the soil from around them until even with the base of your foundation trench. Then work the surface of the rock in with your foundation stone. Continue setting your stakes and string line and digging the foundation along the length of the proposed wall (if longer than 24 feet [7.2 m]).

Laying the Foundation Stones

Choose the stones with the largest surface area and a minimum of 4- to 6-inch (10.2 to 15.2 cm) thickness (though make sure to save your longest stones for through stones). Start at one end of the foundation by laying your first stone with its length running toward the middle of the foundation. The foundation stones should extend from the outside edge into the middle of the foundation at least 12 to 15 inches (30.5 to 38.1 cm) (figure 4, page 43). Lay the most even side of the stone with its outside edge level with your string line. Set the outside edge of the stone as close to the string line as possible without touching it. If the stone touches the line, it'll cause the line to bow slightly, causing the foundation to do the same. You may have to dig down deeper to accommodate thicker stones or add more packed soil underneath thinner ones.

Any large voids beneath a foundation stone should be filled with as big a stone as you can fit into the void. Then wedge in smaller stones to completely fill the void. Wedging beneath a foundation stone should only be done at the end of a stone that's set to the wall's center.

Lay the next foundation stone alongside the previous stone so the stones have as much contact as possible. If necessary, trim the stone to create a tighter fit. Continue setting foundation stones along both sides of the foundation. The overall surface of the completed foundation should be level from side to side and as even as possible.

Carefully fill any spaces left between the foundation stones with the largest stones that will fit in the voids. Then work in smaller stones and rock chips until every space is packed tightly. This process of filling the wall's core is called hearting and is often referred to as the soul of the wall. Packing the core is a deliberate and tedious process that will be done with each course in a free-standing wall.

The Wall's Profile

When building a new wall, "A" frames are needed at both ends of the wall's foundation. "A" frames outline the basic shape of a wall as it's viewed from the wall's end. String lines attached to the frames help gauge the height and width of each course as they taper inward. String lines are critical for keeping the wall's batter true from side to side and from the bottom to the top of the wall.

Building an "A" Frame

"A" frames can be made from wood or metal rods. For wooden frames, use 1 × 4 lumber for the uprights and cross members of the frames. You'll also need two pieces of rebar at least 5 feet (1.5 m) long.

For the 4-foot (1.2 m) high wall, cut two uprights (A) out of the 1 × 4, 40 inches (101.6 cm) long, which will leave a few extra inches at the top of the frame. There are three cross members. The bottom one (B) measures 29 inches (73.7 cm), the middle one (C) measures 23 inches (58.4 cm), and the top one (D) measures 17 inches (43.2 cm) for a wall that's 2 feet (0.6 m) thick at its base.

Lay the two upright pieces (A) out on an even surface. Space the pieces 26 inches (66 cm) apart (representing the width of the wall's base). Make sure the uprights are level, and attach cross member B to the bottom of each upright piece with a single nail on both ends of the cross member. Make a pencil mark at the center of the cross member.

Place one of the pieces of rebar in the center of the frame. (Use the pencil mark on the bottom cross member [B] as a guide.) Measure 3 feet (0.9 m) up from the pencil mark and mark it on the piece of rebar with a piece of tape. Without moving the rebar, place a tape measure opened up to 14 inches (35.6 cm) straight across the tape mark (with the rebar at the center of the measurement). Move the uprights until they meet both sides of the tape measure. This is where you'll attach the top cross member (D). Then attach the middle cross member (C) in the middle of the frame. Repeat for the second frame.

This frame will help your wall maintain the 26-inch (66 cm) base and help ensure your wall tapers to 14 inches (35.6 cm) at the top.

Using the "A" Frame

Stand one "A" frame on top of the foundaton at one end. Directly behind the frame, in the center, drive one of the rebar stakes at least 1 foot (0.3 m) into the ground. To secure the frame in place, tie the frame to the stake (figure 5). With the 2-foot (0.6-m) level set on the top of the frame, level it, which may require shimming underneath one of the legs. Repeat this at the opposite end, then set your string lines taut at the bottom cross members.

Figure 5 An A frame guides the basic shape of a freestanding wall

Wall Ends (Wall Heads)

While the wall tapers from the bottom to the top, the wall ends, also referred to as wall heads, are laid plumb. Wall heads are built with stout, squared cornerstones that are locked together in a dovetail fashion from one course to the next. Laying single cornerstones that are 6 inches (15.2 cm) thick provides the most stable wall end. Complete the wall end by filling in between the cornerstones with smaller face stones. Plumb the wall-end face stones as you build, using the 4-foot (1.2-m) level. If the stones' surfaces are fairly rough, you'll have to take an average reading.

Bottom Courses

Set the first course of the wall using the largest stones left after setting the foundation. Work along one side of the wall for 10 feet (3 m) or so, then work the opposite side. Set the stones parallel to the string line.

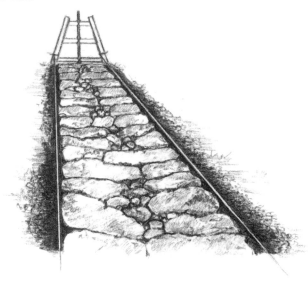

Figure 6 Small stones and rock chips are packed tightly in the voids between the foundation stones.

The Center of the Wall

With each course, the center or heart of the wall will need to be packed solid with smaller stones and rock chips (figure 6). Packing the center tightly is critical for creating a sound wall. After the face stones on both sides have been set, you'll notice open spaces between them. Pack these empty spaces as you did with the foundation, using the largest rocks possible. Then, in the remaining spaces, set smaller rocks and pack rock chips into any voids between the stones until the core is filled as completely as possible. This is a time-consuming process that shouldn't be overlooked.

Wedging

When needed, wedge underneath face stones at the interior of the wall. Avoid wedging stones along the outside face of a wall as much as possible. Walls may settle slightly over time, causing wedges to loosen and fall out, leaving the stone they were supporting with less support.

The Next Courses

Use the string lines as a general guide to match the top of each course. You want to keep the course as close as you can to the height of the string line. Once you have packed the wall's core, you're ready to move the string lines up evenly another 6 inches (15.2 cm). Be sure to check that the string lines are taut and not sagging in the middle.

To avoid running joints (points of structural weakness), break the vertical joints between the stones of your previous course with the stones of the following course. The basic rule of thumb for any stonewall building is "one stone over two and two over one" (see figure 2 on page 41).

The core of this freestanding double-stone wall was carefully packed with smaller stones by students of the Dry Stone Conservancy in Lexington, Kentucky.

Through Stones

Through stones, also referred to as ties, are set out on the course that is midway between the wall's base and the bottom of the capping. Place through stones in the course every 3 to 4 feet (0.9 to 1.2 m) and break the joints of the course they're set on. Through stones that protrude beyond a wall's face by 3 to 4 inches (7.6 to 10.2 cm) provide more strength, and with the extra bit of stone revealed, they become a design element. Once they are laid out, fill in between them with face stones and hearting.

Bond Stones

The wall's upper half will narrow considerably, allowing only medium and smaller stones to be used. It's preferable to have at least 6 to 8 inches (15.2 to 20.3 cm) of each stone extending into the wall for good contact. It's also preferable for long bonding stones to extend into and past the center. Bond stones extend horizontally into and beyond the wall center, binding the two faces of the wall together. Continue setting bond stones in the wall's upper courses. Alternate these stones from side to side to provide further strength to the wall. With bond stones that extend well past the center of the wall, consideration has to be given to the stone that will be set on the opposite side (the shorter stone has to have a minimum depth of 6 inches [15.2 cm]).

Through stones are placed in the course that's at the wall's halfway mark.

Chinking

Chinking stones are small stones used to fill voids in the face of the wall. They're usually set in the wall as an afterthought. Sometimes I find a chink in a pile of scrap that works as is or it may need to be trimmed for a custom fit. The chink should fit far enough into the void so that it won't pop out. When setting a chink, you should be able to push the stone into the void and give it a light tap with the hammer for a snug fit without disturbing the stones around it. Avoid getting carried away with chinking. Sometimes when you step back and look at the total face of a wall, those small voids become shadows that seem to blend in just fine.

A course of stout capstones secures the top of this freestanding, dry-stacked wall.

The Top of the Wall

Traditionally, this style of freestanding wall has a cover course of capstones with a course of coping stones stood vertically in a row on top of the capstones. You may choose to finish your freestanding wall with only a row of capstones and be happy with it. If you choose to cap the wall and leave off the coping, the capstones for this project should be about 3 inches (7.6 cm) thick and 16 inches (40.6 cm) long. Caps of this size completely span the upper surface and allow for a 1-inch (2.5 cm) overhang on each side.

Capstones

Capstones help prevent rainwater from entering the wall's core, so tightly fit the caps together as you lay them. Single stones that completely span the upper surface from side to side are best. When fitting the caps, try to have a 1-inch (2.5 cm) overhang on each side of the wall. Level the caping by using wedges or shims underneath the stones. Making your final course of face stones as level as possible will make leveling the caps much easier.

Coping Stones

Coping stones are set on top of the capstones, if desired. They can be stood up completely vertical or with a 15-degree angle. If a wall is on a slope, the wall copes will slope downhill. These stones can be fairly thin, so it'll take a lot of them to complete the wall.

To start the coping, set a substantial, blocky, cube-shaped stone on top of the wall at one end. The first coping stone will fit snugly against this stone with the others following in a line, like books on a shelf. Coping can be done with single stones that span the width of the wall, in this case 14 inches (35.6 cm). Continue standing the stones to the opposite end of the wall, where you'll need another blocky stone to hold the stones in place.

Set a string line to the average height of your taller coping stones and use the line as a guide. Some taller copes may need to be trimmed, while shorter ones will need to be shimmed.

An even row of neatly stacked single coping stones tops a freestanding double-stone wall rebuilt with salvaged stone by the Dry Stone Conservancy.

To ensure that the stones don't topple off the wall, some of them may need wedges set at one or both of their outer edges. When all the stones are in place, fill in large gaps between the tops of the stones with thin wedge-shaped stones. Lightly tap them into place so they're snug.

Double Copes

Another style of coping is call *double copes*, where two smaller stones are set side by side on top of the capstones. Occasionally, the double copes will overlap slightly where they meet in the center. With double coping stones, it's good to insert a single coping stone every 4 feet (1.2 m) to strengthen the course.

This dry-stacked retaining wall in Hunderton County, New Jersey, is a striking
landscape element. A slight curve in the wall shows off the tightly fit stonework.

A level wall retains the gravel bed in front of this southwestern home.

Retaining Walls

The Theory

The primary purpose of a retaining wall is to retain a bank of soil behind it. Unless the wall is constructed properly, it won't do its job, so before you begin this project, I'll introduce you to the basics of dry-stacked wall construction. As you read this information, refer to the cross section of the finished retaining wall shown on page 52.

Backfill

A dry-stacked retaining wall is built several inches away from the bank it's meant to retain. This distance will vary, depending on the sizes of the stones you set in the wall. When you set a large stone—perhaps 18 inches (46 cm) in depth—you'll leave about 4 inches (10 cm) between its back end and the soil bank. Some of the largest stones that make up the wall's face may be deep enough to extend all the way back to the bank. A stone 6 inches (15 cm) deep, set in the same course, might have an 18-inch (46 cm) space behind it. As you work, you'll fill these spaces with gravel and, if you have any, rubble stones.

Wall Height

The easiest dry-stacked walls to build are generally 2 feet (61 cm) or less in height. These low walls work well for retaining existing low banks of soil or banks cut into sloped areas, but they're sometimes built simply to highlight one portion of a landscape. The photo on this page shows a good example.

Any cut into an earthen bank leaves the exposed soil vulnerable to wind, rain, and frost heaving, and invites the soil to shift. The larger the exposed area, the stouter the retaining wall must be.

Although it's possible to dry-stack retaining walls 5 feet (1.5 m) or taller, you must build them with much larger stones, make them thicker, and increase their batter to 15 degrees. You must also set the stones in the wall's first course slightly farther away from the bank in order to accommodate the wall's extra thickness. Unless you have access to extremely large stones, avoid dry-stacking walls more than 5 feet (1.5 m) in height.

Wall Thickness

The thickness of a dry-stacked retaining wall will vary depending on the sizes of the stones in it and the finished height of the wall. Walls up to 2 feet (61 cm) in height should be about 12- to 20-inches (31 to 51 cm) thick, while walls between 2- and 5-feet (0.6- and 1.5-cm) tall should be 20- to 24-inches (51- to 61-cm) thick.

Batter

Dry-stacked retaining walls are always battered slightly; they lean backward in order to prevent shifting soil in the bank from moving the stones forward and toppling the wall. If you're building a tall wall and don't care for the look of a severe degree of batter, consider making a series of shorter terraced walls, one above the other. (Tips on building terraced walls are provided in chapter 8.) An alternative is a vertical mortared wall, consisting of concrete blocks filled with rebar and concrete, set on a concrete footer, and faced with stucco or stone.

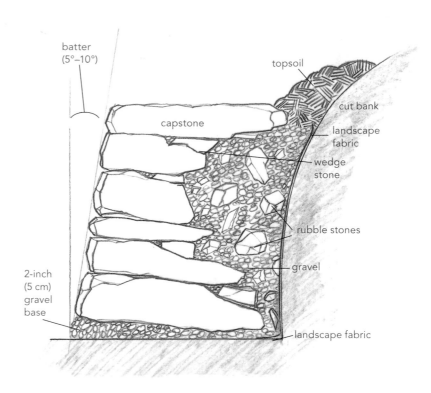

batter (5°–10°)

topsoil

capstone

cut bank

landscape fabric

wedge stone

rubble stones

gravel

2-inch (5 cm) gravel base

landscape fabric

Cross section of a retaining wall.

Stone-Setting Angles

Stones in a dry-stacked retaining wall should be set with their upper surfaces level or pitched slightly toward the back of the wall. This helps maintain the wall's batter and the thrust of the stones against the soil bank.

Upper Surfaces

The illustrations and photographs on page 54 offer three methods for finishing off the top of a wall. If the bank behind your wall is the same height from one end to the other, the wall should be the same height along its entire length so that it follows the line of the bank. The level surface provided by the capstones can serve as a perfect site for potted plants or, if the height is right, as a bench.

A retaining wall 5 feet (1.5 m) or more in height should be built with very large stones. This wall, in the northwestern United States, was stacked with basalt stones.

If the soil bank tapers downward at one end, the wall should do the same. One way to taper a wall is to construct it in "steps" by capping it off at varying heights. To build this type of wall, you'll start at the lowest end of the bank, setting two or three courses of stone from one end of the bank to the other. Then, starting at the low end again, you'll start setting capstones. When you reach the point at which the soil bank rises above the last capstone you've set, you'll stop setting capstones and stack another course or two of stone along the remaining length of the wall. Then you'll set more capstones until the wall needs to step up again, and continue by repeating these steps until the wall is finished.

Another way to construct a tapered wall is to taper the capstones so that they follow the upper surface of the bank itself. The graceful incline created by the sloped capstones offers a beautiful visual effect, but if the taper is a steep one, you won't be able to use the wall as a bench.

The retaining wall above, with its stepped upper surface, consists of a concrete foundation and a block wall faced with mortared quarried stone. This style is known as the "dry-stacked look."

Wall Ends

The stacked ends of a level retaining wall or the tall end of a stepped wall may butt up against another structure such as the foundation of a home. Wall ends may also be freestanding, but keep in mind that freestanding ends are vulnerable, especially if they extend into high-traffic areas. A passing garden cart or climbing children can wreak havoc on their structure, so be especially careful to fit the end stones well.

A low, level wall with wide capstones makes a good place to sit.

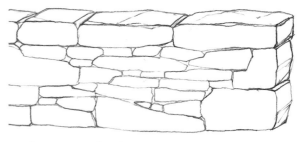

Level retaining wall with squared corners.

A "stepped" retaining wall in progress.

A "stepped" wall, made by setting capstones at different levels, rises to meet the bank behind it.

This wall tapers down with the bank behind it.

A tapered wall is created by reducing its height from one end to the other.

The level gravel driveway in this setting made
an ideal work area for wall building.

On any retaining wall, freestanding ends must have
stone "corners" in order to retain the backfill between
the wall and the soil bank. Corners can be built in a
number of ways. One common method is to combine
two types of stones: block-shaped, chunky stones and a
few longer tie stones that run all the way from the front
face of the wall to the soil bank. Remember that these
tie stones, as well as any other stones that will show at
the front of the wall and around the corner, must have
two adjacent faces.

Another way to construct a corner is to position a
single large, very thick stone on end, at a 90-degree
angle to the face of the wall.

Building a Dry-Stacked Retaining Wall

For several years, I've led stone workshops in my home
state. The one that we photographed for this book took
place at the North Carolina Arboretum at Asheville. Of
the dozen people who registered for this course, only
one had any previous wall-building experience, but we
only needed two separate 8-hour-long workshops to
complete the 60-foot-long (18.3 m) wall pictured on the
next page.

The wall built during the workshop at the Arboretum was low enough to serve as a bench, so we added some backrest stones.

The wall-building instructions you're about to read and the photos that accompany them will walk you through every step we took in the workshop. By the time you've finished this chapter, you'll be ready to build your own dry-stacked retaining wall.

Planning

As in any building project, a little bit of planning and organizing will make your work easier. Before beginning your wall (or any stone project), visualize or sketch the finished structure in its surrounding landscape. You'll need to decide how thick the wall will be, whether it will be straight or curved, and whether it will taper down to the ground or stand squared and level.

The characteristics of your site will play a large role in determining the decisions you make. The workshop retaining wall shown above is 2 feet (61 cm) tall; its height was determined by the cut in the bank behind it. Because this wall is low, it is only 20 inches (51 cm) thick. We used stones up to 18 inches (46 cm) deep. The gravel backfill behind the stone was an average of 2 to 4 inches (5 to 10 cm) deep.

How Much Stone You'll Need

With single dry-stone retaining walls, 1 ton (0.9 t) of stone equals approximately 30 to 35 face feet (9 to 10.5 m) of stonework, depending on the weight of the stone you're using. To calculate the amount of stone for your

By importing soil and encircling it with a low retaining wall, stonemason Frederica Lashley created a planting bed on a level lawn.

project, first determine the total amount of face footage of stonework in the wall. To do this, multiply the proposed wall's length by its height (including the wall ends). Then multiply the capstone's average depth in feet (usually 1½ feet [0.45 m] or so) by the wall's length. Add the two figures for the wall's face footage. For a conservative estimate, divide your total by 30 for the number of tons you'll need to find or order.

For example, if your wall is 20 feet (6 m) long and 3 feet (0.9 m) tall, there will be 60 face feet (18 m) of vertical stonework along the front of the wall. Then, multiply the length by the capstone's average width in feet: $20 \times 1½ = 30$ face feet (9 m). Then, multiply the wall ends' width by their height (say 1½ feet [0.45 m] × 3 feet [0.9 m] = 4½ face

feet [1.4 m] at each end). The total amount of face footage is $60 + 30 + 4½ + 4½ = 99$ face feet, which you can round up to 100 face feet (30 m). Finally, 100 divided by 30 equals 3.3 tons (3 t). So you'll need approximately 3½ tons (3.15 t) of stone for your wall.

If your source for stone is not convenient to your site, I recommend adding an extra half ton of stone to your order for every 3 tons (2.7 t) ordered to ensure plenty of good stone to choose from. Often the preselected pallets of stone in wire baskets or those wrapped with plastic have good building stone but lack larger pieces to use as capstones. Consider buying a pallet of larger pieces for capping material or handpick them from the stone yard's random or select piles.

Selecting and Preparing the Site

Part of a dry-stacked wall's beauty rests in its simplicity; it requires neither mortar nor a concrete footer. It does require, however, a specific site: a mound or bank of soil to retain.

Your land may have an existing bank, a natural berm, or a berm left over from the excavation of your home site. If it doesn't, you'll need to create a berm by importing soil.

Whether you're working with an existing bank or with one you've created, the next step is to make a cut in the soil bank. In order to expedite the workshop, I arranged to have a small loader make the initial cut in our bank. The workshop members then refined the cut by hand, using mattocks and shovels to remove roots and rubble as they worked. Don't worry if you can't afford to use heavy equipment; the initial cut for a low wall can almost always be made by hand. If your soil isn't hard and compact, you can even do this without using a mattock. A shovel works well on looser soils.

As you make the cut, be sure that it angles slightly backward to match the batter of the future wall. Loaders and other pieces of heavy equipment tend to make vertical cuts, so you must take this step even if the major work has already been done for you.

Save about one-quarter of the soil you remove (especially if it's good top soil), placing it just beyond one end of the wall site. When you've finished stacking the wall, you may need this soil to dress out the area between the capstones and the top of the bank. Make a pile of any rubble stones you encounter, too; you'll add them to the gravel backfill.

After you've cut the bank, clean away all debris from the area where the wall will be placed. This surface should be even and free of rubble. Also clear a work area 4 to 6 feet (1.2 to 1.8 m) wide along the length of your site for your tools, piles of large stone, and gravel. Your materials should be as close at hand as possible. Remove any extra soil, adding it to the soil you removed from the cut bank. Like your desk at work or your kitchen counter, the neater you keep this area, the more efficient your labor will be. If you take regular breaks to clean it up, most of the rubble and rock chips you generate will end up mixed into the backfill.

Landscape Fabric

If you live in an area that experiences heavy frost heaving during the winter, you may wish to consider covering the exposed slope with landscape fabric before you begin building. Frost heaving happens when moisture present in the ground freezes and expands, pushing the soil up and outward. In these situations, the soil is often pushed into the wall's gravel backfill and continues moving through to the joints between the stones. If the soil is red clay, this can discolor the stone.

Before you begin building the wall, you may want to cover the cut bank with landscape fabric.

Spread the landscape fabric out against the bank allowing 1 foot (0.3 m) of it to cover the base of the cut and extend the rest to cover the exposed bank. To hold the fabric in place while working, pin it to the top of the bank with a series of nails (16 penny) or use rocks to weigh it down.

Sorting the Stones

After preparing a site, I like to sort my stones by size and sometimes even by shape. Spending the time to do this familiarizes me with the stones I have on hand. I don't remember every one of them, of course, but handling them seems to leave an impression on my subconscious. When I'm building a wall, I often find myself able to locate the perfect stone from the sorted piles.

In regions where severe freezing causes the subsoil to expand, landscape fabric can be used to prevent the soil from pushing through the gravel backfill and into the joints between the stones.

Pay attention to the shapes and faces of the stones as you sort them and leave the most obvious face of each stone facing up. This way, you'll be able to see it when you scan the pile for a certain shape or size. Save the largest, flattest stones in a separate pile; you'll use them as capstones.

Gathering Tools and Materials

Along with your piles of stones, make sure you have a pile of gravel off to one side or waiting in five-gallon (19 l) buckets. You may also want to have several buckets filled with small shim and wedge stones.

Bring out your tools and equipment. Except for items that will rust, everything in a dry-stacked stone project can stay just where it is when you take breaks. The wind isn't likely to blow anything away, and rain won't hurt your materials either. Your project will stay pretty much the way you left it, even if you neglect it for months.

A small loader made the initial cut for this wall. The workshop members then raked soil from the bank's upper surface to fill a few low spots and tamped it down. Exposed roots and rubble stones were removed with shovels and mattocks.

Laying Out the Gravel Bed

For a 2-foot-tall (61-cm) wall, spread out a 2-inch-thick (5-cm) layer of gravel, extending it from the cut bank to a line about 2 inches beyond where the front face of the wall will rest. If you were building a wall 4 feet (1.2 m) tall, with larger stones, you'd need to increase the width of this base by about 4 to 6 inches (10 to 15 cm). At this stage, the width of the gravel bed isn't critical; you can always increase it as you lay out the first course of stone. Use a steel-toothed rake to help spread the gravel evenly.

Setting the First Course of Stone

The first course of stone will carry the weight of the wall. To spread that weight out evenly, select stones with large surface areas. "Large" is a relative term, of course, and will depend on the sizes of the stones available to you.

Set the first stone at one end of the wall site, placing its front edge where you'd like the face of the wall to be. The stone's upper surface should slope slightly down from front to back. Pitching the upper surface of a stone toward the front of the wall, in a direction opposite to the direction of the wall's batter, makes laying the next course more difficult.

Remember that unless the end of your wall butts up against a building foundation, every stone at either end serves as a cornerstone, so it must

Setting the first stone on the gravel bed

Continuing the first course and adjusting a stone's position by pushing gravel underneath it

have two adjacent faces—one that appears at the front of the wall and one that appears around the corner. If this stone doesn't reach all the way back to the soil bank behind it, you must fill the gap by setting another stone directly behind the first one in order to prevent the gravel backfill from filtering out from behind the wall. (Refer to the section entitled "Wall Ends" on pages 53–55 for descriptions of corner-building methods.)

Continue by setting more first-course stones, one by one, working from one end of the wall and stopping a few feet from the other end. Fit the stones as close to each other as possible. (The back ends of the stones don't need to meet perfectly, as any gaps will be filled with gravel, but make every effort to match their front ends well.)

To adjust the stones' angles, add or remove gravel or wedge stones. If points or protrusions keep a particular stone from fitting well with the stone next to it, use a stonemason's hammer and a chisel to trim the stone for a better fit.

Add small stones to make up for the difference in stone thicknesses.

Initial setting of the gravel backfill, using the tapered end of a mason's hammer

This first course is a good place to use stones with one large, flat surface and an opposing surface that is rounded and/or irregular. Position the rounded, irregular surfaces down into the gravel. If necessary, you may even dig down below the gravel and into the soil, in order to set the stones securely and at the desired height.

Now finish the first course by working from the unfinished end of the wall towards the stones you've already set. Why work backward when you're setting these last few feet of stone? Because if you continue forward, especially when you're building a wall that butts up against a solid structure, you'll find yourself struggling to find just the right stone for the very last space, which is often a visual focal point. It's easier to find that last stone first, and then work backward.

If this end of your wall is freestanding, remember that the last stone in every course will serve as a cornerstone.

The stones in the first course don't have to be the same thickness. To make the upper surface of the first course even along its length, just add shim stones or smaller stones on top of the shorter ones you've already set. When you've finished, stand at one end and check the overall appearance of this course to make sure that the stones are where you want them to be.

Spreading and Setting the Gravel Backfill

If you have rubble stones, scatter some of them in the void behind the first course. Then spread gravel over them and into any gaps around the back edges of the first-course stones. Now you must set the gravel around the sides and backs of the wall stones in order to level and lock them in place. (The mortar in a mortared wall locks the stones in a similar fashion.) Gravel setting is a tedious job, but it strengthens a wall considerably.

Stone chips plug the gaps between stones in a course in order to prevent the backfill from spilling out.

An elegant retaining wall built with block-shaped stones

When filling large voids with gravel, I sometimes use the handle of my hammer before setting the gravel with a length of rebar.

Setting gravel behind the capstones with a tire iron

The thin shim stone set between the two larger stones is used to level the top stone.

I use a piece of rebar, with one rounded end, as a setting tool. A short crowbar or the long, tapered end of a mason's hammer will also work well. Jab the tool into the gravel around the backs and sides of the wall stones, forcing the gravel into the voids. If, as you do this, the gravel disappears into a void beneath a stone, add more gravel or pull some forward from the backfilled area and continue setting it until the void is filled.

Before setting the next course, brush back any gravel remaining on top of the first course stones; the first few inches of the top surface of every stone should be bare. Gravel on these upper front surfaces will prevent the stones in the next course from making good contact.

Splitting away protruding layers of stone, bit by bit, to create a smooth surface.

Dry-Stacking the Remaining Courses

To complete the remaining courses, you'll repeat the very same steps: laying the stones in each course and then adding and setting the gravel-and-rubble backfill. As you work, keep the following tips in mind:

- Pay attention to the wall's batter as you work. After setting every couple of courses, stand at one end of the wall, so that you're looking down its length. The slope of the wall should be 5 to 10 degrees. (If you're not very familiar with degrees, look at a clock set at 12:01. The minute hand will rest at a 6-degree angle in relation to the hour hand. The batter of your wall should look very much the same.)

- Remember to complete the last few feet of each course by setting the corner or end stone first and then working backward toward the stones you've already set.

- The key to building a fine wall is ensuring small joints by getting the surfaces of each stone to make as much contact as possible with the surfaces of the stones around it. Take your time choosing stones. When a stone looks like it will fit well in a particular spot, place it there. Sometimes, flipping the stone, end over end, may make it fit even better. If necessary, trim away small protrusions or thin tapering edges to make stones fit more tightly.

- On occasion, you'll need to add a wedge stone to stabilize a larger stone, or a thin shim stone to adjust its overall height.

- There are no strict guidelines for setting these particular stones. They are most useful in strengthening the wall after setting a number of smaller stones that don't reach back into the wall very far.

Adjusting the wall height to prepare for the next capstone.

Setting the backrest stones in place.

Through stones can be long and rectangular, or they can also be long, wide, flat, thin stones similar to capstones, yet not thick enough to be a capstone. For a retaining wall, any stone that reaches well back into the wall's interior can be considered a through stone.

- Always keep the next course in mind as you lay the one beneath it. If a stone has major protrusions that will present problems when you lay the next course, trim them before placing the stone in the wall.

- Always try to break the joints of the previous course. That is, position your stones to cover the joints between the stones in the course beneath. The rule of thumb here is "two-stones-over-one, one-over-two, two-over-one," and so on. Sometimes, when particular stones fit together exceptionally well, I skip this rule of thumb, but not often and never for more than two courses. If the joints break in the same places, course after course, you'll end up with running joints—vertical spaces running through more than a single course. These create potential weak areas in the wall, as well as being visually obvious. Adding a stretcher is one way to break several joints with a single stone.

- Because the final course of your wall—the capstone course—will bring your wall to its finished height, you'll need to do a few quick calculations in order to decide how many courses of stone to set before capping the wall off. The next section explains how.

This wall, made with quarried boulders weighing from 300 pounds (136 kg) to 2 tons (1.8 t) by master mason Jim Morris, tapers down with a series of stepped capping stones to meet a single boulder at the wall's end.

These courses of rounded glacial erratics are stepped back severely to create the wall's batter.

The Top of the Wall

There are three styles for finishing off the top of a dry-laid retaining wall. The top surface of the wall will be capped with capstones, which, in this case, are usually the largest stones with two fairly flat surfaces. If the bank of soil is the same height from one end of the wall to the other, then the surface of the capstones will be level from end to end. If, however, the soil bank gradually tapers downward at either end, the wall should do the same.

Stepped Wall

One way to taper a wall end is to construct it in "steps" by capping it off at varying heights. To build this way, you'll start at the lowest end of the bank, running two or three courses of stone from one end of the wall to the other. Then, starting at the low end again, you'll begin setting capstones. When you reach the point at which the soil bank rises above the last capstone you've set, you'll stop setting capstones and stack another course or two along the remaining length of the wall. Then you'll set more capstones until the wall needs to step up again. Continue by repeating these steps until the wall is finished.

Tapered Wall

If the bank tapers at one or both ends, the graceful taper of the wall can be accentuated by allowing the capstones to follow that tapering line. This means the capstones will be sloped with the tapering end.

Laying Capstones

Properly set capstones are a protective course that prevents the wall stones from loosening. Your goals are to make sure these stones sit securely on the ones beneath them and to match their edges as closely as possible. Setting the capstones can be challenging, time-consuming work, particularly if you want the

Trimming a protrusion from the edge of a capstone will reduce the gap between capstones and ensure a tighter fit.

These capstones are set at relatively the same height using the contour of the bank to determine the finished height of the wall.

Set smaller capstones between and behind larger ones to conserve your supply of large stones.

Selecting and matching stones for a bench backrest

Workshop participants enjoying their bench.

wall to be level from end to end. If the finished wall is going to be 3 feet (0.9 m) tall and your capstones average 4 to 6 inches (10.2 to 15 cm) thick, start laying them when the courses of wall stone have reached 28 inches (71.1 cm) high. If you build up too high, you may have to take wall stones out in order to set the capstone at the correct height. The tricky part of capping comes from finding just the right stone or group of stones to fit underneath each capstone. It's easier to have a capstone selected and build up to match its thickness with the finished height of the wall.

If the wall is going to be level from one end to the other, you can start capping at either end. If the wall is stepped up with the grade of the bank, you'll need to start at the lowest end of the grade for the wall's end. Choose a capstone that also works as a wall end. Build the courses and wall end and set the capstone you've chosen. You may have to set one or two more at this level. Continue setting the wall ends, facing stones, and

capstones until the grade steps up. Here you'll have to build another wall end and take the wall courses up at the same time. Continue stepping up until you reach the wall's finished height, and then set the remaining capstones level to the opposite end of the wall.

If you have a limited number of large capstones, consider staggering them and filling in between with the next largest stone. Once set, a capstone should be level along the length of the wall (unless it's at a tapering end) and have a slight slope to its surface from the wall's face back to the bank. Thoroughly pack underneath each capstone with pea gravel as you set them, then move on to the next one.

Large stones with only one flat surface can be used as capstones. Set the flat surface down on the upper course of wall stone so it has good contact. The other irregular surface will be the top of the wall. Capping with an irregular surface on top gives plenty of visual texture to the wall's upper surface.

Profile of a double-stone retaining wall

Making a Bench Backrest

If you want your wall to serve as a bench, consider adding a stone backrest. These stones not only provide comfortable back support, but also help retain any portion of the soil bank that rises above the finished wall.

First, select a few capstone-sized stones, each with one fairly even surface. In order to match their edges, position them on the ground, setting them on end and bracing them against 5-gallon (19 l) buckets filled with gravel or stones. When you've found a combination that works, set these backrest stones on the back edges of the wall capstones, leaning them against the soil bank at an angle.

Final Touches

The area just behind the capstones on a retaining wall is a fine one for planting. Cover the visible backfill material with the soil that you set aside when you started and top-dress the soil with mulch. Brush away any loose crushed stone or soil when you're finished. Then take the rest you deserve!

Double Retaining Walls

Double dry-stone retaining walls are superior in strength to single stone ones and should be considered when building walls taller than 5 feet (1.5 m) or for securing extremely unstable banks of soil.

The profiles of a double dry-stone retaining wall and a freestanding stone wall (page 42) reveal many similarities. Use the directions given for building a dry-stacked freestanding wall for building a double-stone retaining wall, keeping the following considerations in mind:

- A double-stone retaining wall will use almost twice as much stone as a single-stone wall.
- Build up the interior and exterior courses at the same time and tie them together using bond and through stones.
- Only the exterior face is battered with a 1:6 slope from the base to the top; the interior wall is laid plumb.
- Add backfill between the exposed bank and the interior wall as each course is completed.
- Cap the wall the same as a single-stone retaining wall.

CHAPTER FOUR

DRY-LAID PAVING AND PATHS

Paved areas and paths encourage us to linger, lounge, and enjoy our natural surroundings. Start with a stepping-stone path or simple paved entryway. Once you've had some practice dry-laying stones, a world of projects awaits your elegant patios, beautiful courtyards, welcoming walkways, and more.

With dry-laid paving projects you won't have the extra expense of concrete and mortar. A good selection of stone set on a gravel base makes a durable attractive surface ready for years of enjoyment. Those bare spots of ground around the house that get a lot of foot traffic are perfect for a paving project. You could create a simple stone path to cover those dozen steps made so often to the recycling bins and trashcans. Or you could pave a landing at the bottom of the steps off the deck or the stoop at the back door. A larger-scale project might be a dry-laid patio.

Selecting Stone

Paving stones need one surface that's fairly even and coarse (for good traction). They also need to be of a thickness relative to the size of its surface area. For dry-laid paving, stones with a small surface area of 6 square inches (39 cm²) and smaller (used to fill in between larger stones) will need a thickness of at least 6 inches (15.2 cm) to be set securely in a base of pea gravel or rock dust. Stones with a surface area of 6 to 12 square inches (39 to 78 cm²) should have a minimum thickness of 4 inches (10.2 cm). Pavers with surface areas 1½ square feet (117 cm²) and larger can have a minimum thickness of 2 inches (5.1 cm).

Stones with edges that are squared rather than sloped or tapered are best. Often, a tapered surface can be easily trimmed with a hammer. If you're paving with fieldstone or random quarried stone, the stones' thicknesses can vary quite a bit. If paving with stones of a more uniform size, choose pieces of cut flagstone that measure 2 to 3 inches (5.1 to 7.6 cm) thick and 1½ square feet (117 cm²) or larger.

Avoid using stones with smooth surfaces, such as polished granite or marble. Stones that are extremely soft should be skipped over as well; they won't hold up to much wear and are likely to flake off and become a nuisance.

How Much Stone You'll Need

Figuring the amount of stone needed depends largely upon the average thickness of the stone. Large slabs of random or cut sandstone, 3 inches (7.6 cm) thick, will pave roughly 75 square feet (6.8 m²) per ton (0.9 t). With pieces of field or quarried stone averaging 4 to 6 inches (10.2 to 15.2 cm) thick, 1 ton (0.9 t) will pave 40 to 50 square feet (3.6 to 4.5 m²).

Fieldstone Entryway and Courtyard

This project, an entryway-and-courtyard combination, consists of fieldstone pavers set on a gravel bed. As you can see in the two photos on the next page, the entryway portion runs between one exterior wall of a house and a mortared, concrete-block retaining wall faced with stone. I've chosen this as a first project because once you understand how to build it, you'll be able to construct almost any other dry-laid paving project.

Selecting and Defining the Site

A freestanding paved area—one that doesn't sit next to an existing structure—is very easy to build. Paved areas that abut building foundations are a bit more complex and require some careful thought during the planning stages. Why? Because you must make sure that rainwater doesn't drain toward the building or splash up under the building's siding. Unless you grade the site properly, water may damage the siding and flood your basement or crawl space.

This fieldstone entryway, at Herb Mountain Farm (Weaverville, North Carolina), extends around one corner of a house to form a small courtyard.

To redirect rainwater, most sites next to buildings only need to be graded so that water flows away from the foundation. You'll find out how to do this in the next section. Sites that are difficult to grade properly may require an added drainage system. Installing these can be time consuming, but if you're willing to spend the time rather than switching to another site, use the drainage-system tips provided in this chapter.

Once you've selected a possible site, visualizing the finished paving project is much easier if you lay out its perimeters. For square or rectangular areas, use string lines to define the edges. Pound stakes into the soil at each corner and tie strings from one to another, keeping the strings close to the ground. For more organic shapes, lay out a garden hose or outline the site with sprinkled lines of corn meal. Then familiarize yourself with the results for a few days, making any adjustments you like before you begin work.

Protecting Siding

To prevent rainwater from splashing up from the pavers and touching the siding on the structure, the tops of the stones closest to the building should be at least 6 inches (15 cm) below the bottom of the siding. (Building codes in many areas specify this distance.)

First, remove any sod from the site. Then, to ensure that the ground next to the structure is low enough, make the following calculation:

> Average thickness of your fieldstone pavers
> + 4 inches (10 cm) for the gravel bed underneath them
> + 6 inches (15 cm) from the tops of the pavers to the siding
> _____
> = Required distance between the soil and the bottom of the siding

Now measure the distance between the soil and siding at your site. If this distance isn't equal to or greater than the result of the calculation above, you'll have to remove some soil. Before you do this, read the next section.

If you just can't obtain the necessary clearance, use the following method to protect your siding. Dig a 4-inch-deep (10.2 cm), 4-inch-wide trench in the soil next to the foundation and fill the trench with gravel. Rather than setting your paving stones right next to the foundation, you'll set them along the outer edge of this trench.

Determining the "Pitch"

A paving site next to a building must be pitched (or sloped) so that water will run down and away from the building foundation. Grading the soil to create this pitch is less critical with freestanding paved areas. If these are located on poorly drained soil, however, they should be pitched to direct water from the site.

The standard pitch for paving projects is at least ⅛ inch (3 mm) per linear foot (30 cm) of paving and never more than ¼ inch (6 mm) per foot. What does this mean? That for every foot of paving, measured from the high point of the site to its low point, the paved surface must slope ⅛ inch downward.

To calculate the overall pitch for your site, first determine the direction in which you'd like rainwater to flow. (Always direct water away from building foundations.) Next, measure the distance from the edge of the site that should be highest (in this case, at the building foundation) to the outermost edge of the site, running your tape measure in the desired direction of water flow.

Now multiply ⅛ by that length. If, for example, your site measures 8 feet (2.4 m) from the building foundation out to the edge, multiply ⅛ by 8. The result, 1 inch (2.5 cm), is the required pitch. The soil at your site must be 1 inch higher at the foundation than it is at the far edge.

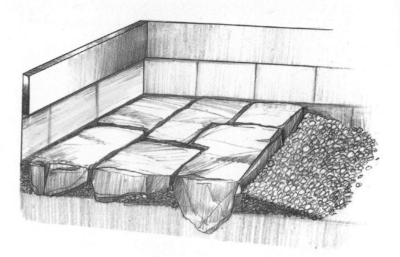

Fieldstone pavers on a gravel bed.

Grading the Site

To create the correct pitch at your site, you'll probably need to add or remove soil from some areas. Use a mattock, a shovel with a square blade, and a wheelbarrow to remove soil. To build up the soil, first add a layer of damp subsoil (damp soil is easier to compact), no more than 6 inches (15 cm) thick. Tamp the soil down well, using a commercial, hand-held tamping tool or a homemade substitute. Repeat this process, adding subsoil in layers, until the desired height is achieved. If your site is 200 square feet (18.6 m) or more, you may want to rent a gas-operated tamper. Be sure to wear earplugs when using this machine!

Keeping track of the pitch as you grade the site is less critical than monitoring the pitch of the paving stones as you set them, but it's a good idea to check the soil after grading it. Stand at the outermost edge of the site and kneel or lie down so that your eyes are at ground level. From that vantage point, you should be able to see a slight incline all the way up to the building foundation (or to the high point of a freestanding site).

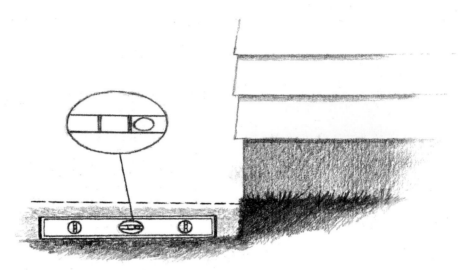

The bubble in the level's vial should look similar to this illustration, if the ground below the pavers has been pitched properly.

A more accurate way to monitor the pitch is to use a level; a 4-foot-long (1.2 m) model works best. First, set the level on any level surface. Then lift up one end to the proper pitch position. With a 4-foot-long level, for example, lift one end up exactly ½ inch (13 mm); hold a 2-foot-long (61 cm) level up ¼ inch (6 mm). With the level supported in this position, use an indelible marker to mark two lines on the level's vial, one on each side of the air bubble inside it. Then, as you grade the site, periodically rest the level on the ground and adjust the soil until the bubble rests between these two marks. (Make sure when you set your level down on the soil or pavers that it's pointing in the right direction, or you'll end up with a pitch directed toward the foundation instead of away from it!)

Improving Drainage

Good drainage is important, especially in regions that get a lot of rain and snow. When water-logged soil underneath stone pavers freezes, it can cause the soil to heave upward, displacing the pavers as it does.

To test the drainage at your site, dig a 2- to 3-foot-deep (61- to 91- cm) hole and fill it with water. If the water hasn't drained away within several hours, the soil in that area doesn't drain well.

If the soil at your site is heavy clay and the site is properly graded, poor drainage shouldn't be a problem. The clay soil will shed water that drains down through the gravel bed, and the pitch of the slope will send this water away. If the soil just beneath the pavers is spongy, however, and rests on compacted subsoil, the spongy soil will absorb water and the subsoil will prevent it from draining downward. One remedy for this problem is to cover the soil with a 2-inch-thick (5 cm) layer of clay soil and top it with a tamped layer of road bond. These compacted layers will help shed water that seeps down through the gravel bed above them.

Drainage problems are also common in two other situations. If the soil at the low edge of a properly pitched site doesn't drain well, water may accumulate in that area. Water will also stand at the low edge of a site if it has nowhere else to flow. The best way to

Japanese Surface Drains

The attractive Japanese surface drain shown in this photo rests in the center of a paved area that extends under and around an open carport. Because the carport was designed without gutters, the drain was positioned to catch water from the roof and carry it away.

To create this drain, the mason wrapped a length of perforated pipe and set it into a trench running directly beneath the drip edge of the carport roof. Next, he covered the pipe with several inches of gravel. To direct water down through the gravel and into the pipe, he then set small stones into the gravel, positioning them on edge and side by side.

deal with these kinds of problems is to install one or more simple French drains—gravel-filled trenches that are positioned to catch water from the paved area and pitched to carry it away. Sometimes, lengths of perforated plastic pipe, 4 to 6 inches (10 to 15 cm) in diameter, are set at the bottoms of these trenches. (Perforated pipe, which has a solid bottom and slits along its top, is available at home-improvement centers in short lengths that lock together, or in longer rolls.)

Figuring out where to place a drainage system will depend on the nature of your paving project and may require the advice of a landscape architect. As a general rule, the trench should catch water as it flows from the site and should be pitched to carry the water away. Study the graded site carefully to determine the direction of water flow.

To install a perforated-pipe drainage system, start by digging a 12-inch-deep (30 cm) trench, with a pitch of about ¼ inch (6 mm) per foot. Position the trench to catch runoff from the paved area and extend it far enough beyond the site to ensure that it won't release water nearby. Next, to prevent sediment from filling the pipe, wrap it with landscape fabric, tying the fabric in place with string or wire. Place the wrapped pipe in the trench, with its solid half facing down and the perforations facing up. Then fill the trench with gravel. (Note that because the ¼-inch-per-foot pitch of the trench and pipe will be greater than the ⅛-inch-per-foot pitch of your graded site, the slope of the trench will be greater than that of the pitched site.)

Maintaining a Paved Area

Even if you've carefully removed every speck of sod from a paving site and have covered the soil with landscape fabric, you may have some unwanted plant growth in the paved area. Airborne seeds have a way of settling into the joints. If you don't enjoy spraying weed-killing chemicals (I don't), keep a vigilant watch for unwanted seedlings and pull them out while they're still young. If you enjoy the informal look that plant growth can lend to paving, consider setting out attractive creeping varieties; these will help crowd out less desirable plants. (See chapter 6 for details.)

Setting Borders around Pitched Sites

Unless the lowest edge of a pitched paving site has a border, the gravel at the outer edge will migrate in the direction of the slope. You may either set your borders before spreading the gravel or, if it isn't critical to you exactly where the borders are situated, you may wait to set them until just before setting the last pavers at the outer edge of the site. Following are some tips on borders:

- If the ground just beyond the low edge of your site slopes steeply, a low, dry-stacked retaining wall at the edge of the paved area makes an excellent border. Construct the wall so the pavers along the rim of the site also serve as the wall's capstones.
- Block-shaped chunks of stone make good borders. Sink these stones into the soil at the rim of the paving site and cap them with the outermost pavers or, to add more definition to the rim, choose border

stones tall enough to rise above the paved surface. You may need to fill the gaps in the vertical joints by inserting chinking stones, or gravel will leak from between the border stones.

- Squared timbers, anchored with lengths of rebar, make visually pleasing borders for sites with straight edges. These should be set on 2-inch-thick (5-cm) gravel beds placed along the site's exterior edges, with their upper surfaces just above ground level. The paving stones should meet their interior edges. Start by digging trenches around the site, making them deep enough to hold both the layer of gravel and the timbers. Then drill 1/2-inch-diameter (13-mm) holes through each timber, spacing the holes 2 to 3 feet (61 to 91 cm) apart. Spread the gravel in the trenches and position the drilled timbers on the gravel. Then drive 2-foot (61-cm) lengths of 1/2-inch-diameter (1.3 cm) rebar through each hole and into the ground beneath the layer of gravel. You may either set the lengths of rebar flush with the tops of the timbers, or sink them and plug the holes with wooden plugs.

Setting Borders around Level Sites

Gravel won't migrate from a freestanding paved area that is flat and level, but a border will help define the site visually. If the border material doesn't have too many joints, it will also help discourage surrounding vegetation from creeping into the paved area.

Suitable border materials for level sites include long, squared timbers; lengths of steel edging, 1/4 inch (6 mm) thick and 4 inches (10 cm) tall; stone slabs, about 2 inches (5 cm) thick and 8 inches (20 cm) tall, set on their ends; bricks; and Belgian blocks. To prevent borders from acting as obstacles to lawn mowers and feet, set their upper surfaces at or just above ground level.

This two-level patio is paved with quarried stones set in a random design.

Rounded river rocks complement a single stone step at the edge of a courtyard paved with fieldstone.

Spreading the Gravel Bed

After grading the site and setting the borders, spread a 2- to 4-inch-thick (5- to 10-cm) gravel bed over the soil. (You may set the borders later if you like.) Consider spreading a layer of landscape fabric over the soil first and distributing the gravel on top of it. The fabric will prevent any grass from springing up through your pavers.

If your pavers are more than 3 inches (8 cm) thick, spread a 2-inch-thick (5-cm) bed of gravel. If the stones are thinner than 3 inches, spread a 4-inch-thick (10-cm) gravel bed. The gravel will help define the site visually as you work. It will also help keep the site from turning into a mud bath if it rains before you're able to finish the project.

As well as helping water to drain away, the gravel bed makes it easier to adjust the pitch of each paving stone. Even if you live in an arid region, where moisture isn't a problem, it's much easier to adjust pavers that sit on top of gravel than it is to position them properly in soil.

If you choose to use concrete pavers, bricks, cobbles, wood rounds, flagstones—or a combination of paving stones and any of these materials—see pages 80–81 for instructions on adapting this gravel bed.

Laying Out the First Pavers

Start placing the paving stones at one end of the foundation. If your paving site meets an inside corner, where two foundation walls or a wall and outdoor steps meet, set the first paver in the 90-degree corner. Finding a stone with a 90-degree corner will be easy at this point because the size of the stone won't matter. If you wait until you've set the surrounding stones, you'll have to search for a cornerstone that is just the right size to fit a defined space. (Being this meticulous isn't necessary, but the eye is naturally drawn to corners, and a neat corner will enhance the overall appearance of your work.)

Continue by laying out a row of pavers along the edge of the foundation, leaving ¾- to 1-inch-wide (1.9 to 2.5 cm) gaps between the stones. The edges of these stones don't necessarily need to meet the building foundation. You can always fill any gaps with gravel, rounded river rock, or small pieces of stone.

As you lay out the first few pavers, you may need to add or remove gravel to adjust their heights. Don't forget that the upper surface of each stone must be a minimum of 6 inches (15 cm) below the bottom edge of the siding. Also keep in mind that although the pavers should be pitched away from the foundation, each stone must be level from side to side (parallel to the foundation). Check each one with a level after it's in place. Because fieldstones typically have irregular surfaces, your level will never sit perfectly flat, of course, so hold the level to compensate for bumps and dips on the stone surfaces.

When you've finished laying out the first row of stones, set a straight, 8- to 10-foot-long (2.4 to 3 m) 2 × 4 on its narrow edge, across the stone surfaces and parallel to the foundation. Then kneel down and check to see that the bottom edge of the 2 × 4 meets the stone surfaces as evenly as possible. Pay particular attention to the upper surfaces next to joints between stones. When these surfaces don't meet along the same plane, make adjustments by adding gravel under the low stone while gently prying it up with a pry bar. To lower a high spot, remove gravel from beneath the stone. (Sometimes, stamping on a high stone's edge will settle it.)

Continue laying out stones until you've completed two or three rows, checking each row with the 2 × 4 as you complete it. Also use your level to check the pitch.

Filling Joints

After setting the first few rows of pavers, fill the joints between the stones with gravel. Then settle the gravel by poking it with a metal rod. The goal here is to distribute the gravel evenly underneath the stones. To make sure you're filling all the voids beneath and between the stones, stand on top of each stone as you work, gently shifting your weight from side to side and moving your body around in a complete circle. When a paver rocks as you do this, use your metal rod to rework the gravel until the stone is stable. When you're finished, make sure that none of the gravel remains on the upper surfaces of the pavers.

Use your 2 × 4 and level to recheck the stone surfaces periodically and make height adjustments as necessary. As you continue, if you run into an area that looks perfect for a plant, don't set the gravel in it. Instead, remove all the gravel from that gap. (Instructions for selecting and setting out plants can be found in chapter 6.)

Setting the Remaining Pavers

Before setting the remaining stones, study the photos on pages 82–83. They'll provide you with some very useful information. Some of the fieldstone pavers shown, which were handpicked during several trips to a stone yard, weigh 200 pounds (91 kg) each. You might want to choose smaller stones for a first project! After we transported these pavers to the building site, we moved them all by hand through a narrow passageway to our small courtyard paving site. We were able to stand some of the squared or rounded stones on edge and "walk" them back to the site. The others we carried (working in teams of two people) or transported in a wheelbarrow.

After setting a few rows of pavers, lay out the stones that abut the borders. This is a good place to set stones with less than perfect surfaces, such as those with tapering edges. (If your site is freestanding and doesn't have borders, set tapered stones with their tapered edges at the outer rim.)

Next, position a long 2 × 4 to span the gap between these perimeter stones and the other pavers to see whether the outer stones are positioned at heights that will ensure a correct pitch for the completed project. Make any necessary adjustments to the outer stones. Then continue setting the remaining pavers, working from the previously paved section out toward the perimeter stones.

If your borders aren't in place yet, set them now, and then set the remaining pavers. When all the stones are in place, lie down at the outer edge of the paved area, with your eyes at its surface level, and check the paving for dips or high spots. Also make a final check with your 2 × 4 and level. Fill the remaining joints with gravel and set it well; remember that the gravel mustn't rise above the pavers' surfaces. Sweep any stray gravel back into the joints and hose the surface down to clean it up. Invite some friends over to enjoy the finished project!

Estimating Required Quantities

For dry-laid flagstone paving projects, about 1 ton of stone will cover 75 square feet (7 m²).

Filling Joints with Other Materials

If coarse gravel isn't visually appealing to you, don't fill the joints completely. Instead, set only a little gravel in each one, leaving an empty channel about 2 inches (5 cm) deep. After you've set all the pavers, fill in these channels with pea gravel, coarse sand, or rock dust. Pea gravel is set in the same way as coarse gravel—with a metal rod. To set sand or rock dust, soak it thoroughly with water. After the soaked material seeps down into the gravel bed, you may need to add more and soak the joints again. Keep these finer materials at least ½ inch (13 mm) below the upper surfaces of the pavers.

If you're working with a combination of stone pavers and thinner paving materials such as bricks, concrete pavers, or faux stones, fill the joints with rock dust or coarse sand rather than gravel.

Purchasing an extra ¼ ton (254 kg) of stone for every 2 tons (2034 kg) you think you'll need will not only save you extra trips to the stone yard, but will also allow you to pick the best stones as you build. Just stack any leftover stones (or culls) in a corner of your yard until you're ready to tackle another project or until a friend or neighbor, inspired by your efforts, wants to do some stonescaping of his or her own.

Paving

▲ Use a long level to check the pitch from one stone to another. The same tool works well for checking the relative heights of two stones.

▲ To bring one paver closer to another, first remove some of the gravel between them. The tapered end of a brick mason's hammer works well for this purpose.

▲ To move a large paver, jab a pry bar underneath its edge. Then push up and against the bar to move the stone.

▲ A pry bar also helps when you're making minor adjustments to a stone's position.

▲ Use a blacksmith's hammer to break off unwanted protrusions from a fieldstone paver.

▲ Take the time to check the fit of each stone.

▲ Trim away small protrusions that prevent a good fit.

▲ The more care you take fitting the stones, the better the paving will look.

▲ To adjust the height of a thin stone, add gravel beneath it.

▲ Before positioning a large, thick stone, compare its thickness with the thickness of the stones that will surround it.

▲ The wide blade of a mattock makes a good lever when adjusting the height of a large stone.

▲ Some fieldstones can be split in order to reduce their thickness.

▲ You may need to rake away some gravel before setting especially thick stones.

▲ Use a shovel to guide gravel into the joints.

▲ Use the tapered end of a mason's hammer to begin setting the gravel in the joints.

▲ Set the gravel thoroughly by using a metal rod.

▲ A hand broom helps brush gravel into the joints as you work.

Trimming Flagstone Pavers

Because flagstone is sedimentary and tends to separate along its layers, trimming it across the grain requires a special technique.

First define the portion to be removed by using a straightedge and chisel to score a line across the face of the stone. Prop the stone up at a tilt, with the marked line at the lower end. Position a hose with a nozzle at the top of the stone so that you can direct a slow, steady stream of water down the stone and across the scored line. Put on your safety glasses and ear plugs.

Next, using a double-insulated circular saw with an abrasive blade, you must cut a straight, shallow groove, ¼ inch (6 mm) deep, along the scored line. Position the front edge of the baseplate on top of the stone, with the saw's guide mark over the scored line. Hold the saw at an angle so the blade doesn't touch the stone. Turn the saw on, carefully lower the spinning blade down until it touches the start of the scored line, and guide the saw gently back and forth. Don't exert any downward pressure on the blade; instead, allow the weight of the saw to do the cutting. If you need to lift the blade guard in order to keep track of the cut, do so, but be extremely careful! The water flowing over the stone will reduce dust in the air as well as wear on the blade.

Two important warnings here: Make absolutely sure that your circular saw is double-insulated before you run water anywhere near it. Also, if you've plugged the saw into an extension cord, waterproof the joint where the cord and the saw plug meet by wrapping it tightly with duct tape.

Now set the stone on the gravel bed of your paving site, with the scored side facing up. To raise the stone slightly, position a section of 2 × 4 underneath the portion of the stone you want to save, aligning one edge of the board with the groove in the stone. Keep as much

Using a circular saw to score a flagstone paver.

of the stone as possible in contact with the gravel; this will help the stone absorb the shock when you strike it with a hammer. The portion of the stone you want to remove should now be raised above the gravel bed.

Using a 2- to 3-pound (0.9 to 1.4-kg) hammer, strike the portion of the stone you wish to remove. If this portion is especially long, use two hammers simultaneously, holding one in each hand. In most cases, the stone will break cleanly along the groove. If only one layer breaks off, score, cut, and break off the remaining material.

Flagstone Patio

Paving with flagstone is very similar to paving with fieldstone, but flagstone work has one distinct advantage: It's easier to find flagstones that are close to equal in thickness. It is also relatively simple to cut and trim

Assorted stone sizes, varied "grain" in the stones, and a range of colors make this small flagstone patio an especially attractive spot. Exterior lighting along one edge helps ensure safe nighttime use. The seedlings along the base of the timber wall will eventually fill in this border area.

flagstone to a specific size and shape. A flagstone paver works best when it's at least 1½ feet (46 cm) square and 1½ to 3 inches (4 to 8 cm) thick. Thinner flagstones will hold up in mortared paving projects, but not in dry laid ones. And remember: The smaller the stone, the thicker it should be. Large flagstones should be around 1½ to 2 inches (4 to 5 cm) thick; smaller flagstones should be about 3 inches thick.

Setting the Border

Start by removing any sod from the site and grading the area as you would for any paving project. For help selecting a border material for a flagstone paving project, refer to page 78. Set the borders after grading the site.

Once set, the border material will define the perimeter of the project and will help retain the bed of gravel underneath it.

Spreading the Gravel Bed

Spread a 2-inch-thick (5-cm) layer of gravel over the exposed soil to ensure a mud-free work area. After I spread the gravel for this project, I stood most of the pavers on edge, leaning them against the timber retaining wall to make them easier to scan as I made my selections.

Laying the Pavers

As with any paving project that abuts one or more existing structures, you should work outward from the structures. If one end of your site is enclosed on three sides, start at that end, setting the first stone at an interior corner. Then line up two or three stones on the gravel, next to the cornerstone, matching their edges as closely as possible and adjusting their heights by adding or removing gravel.

Experiment with the paving layout by positioning a few stones on the gravel bed.

If your site has an inside corner, always lay out the cornerstone first.

Next, working one stone at a time, flip each stone back and, using a trowel, spread a 1½-inch-thick (4-cm) layer of rock dust or coarse sand over the gravel. Reposition the stone on top of this bed, removing or adding rock dust or sand as necessary to adjust its height. To prevent the rock dust or sand from settling into the gravel, some masons add a 2-inch-thick (5-cm) layer of tamped road bond between the gravel bed and the layer of sand or rock dust. If you choose to do this, tamp the gravel down thoroughly before adding the road bond.

Your goal as you continue to lay out the flagstone pavers is to fit the larger stones together as closely as possible. As you do this, you may need to trim one or two small sections off some of the stones and larger sections off others.

Paving the site section by section is easiest. Arrange several pavers on the gravel bed to cover an area about 5 feet (1.5 m) square, matching their edges and trimming them as necessary. Then, one by one, flip these stones back, spread the rock dust or sand beneath them, and lower them back down again, adjusting their heights as you work.

As you lay out the stones, you'll end up with small empty pockets here and there; fill these with smaller stone pavers. Because small pieces of flagstone tend to shift, use heavier, thicker pieces of fieldstone or quarried stone for this job, each about 4 to 6 inches (10 to 15 cm) thick. Alternatively, you may fill these gaps by positioning small, thin stones with flat even edges vertically. Small pockets are also great locations for colorful stones and ones with interesting shapes.

Small stones are especially useful when you need to fill voids between large pavers, but they must be thick, or they'll shift.

After setting each stone on its rock-dust bed, check its height and pitch in relation to the pavers around it.

After setting each stone, use a level to check its pitch. Also check to see that each stone is level from side to side. To check the evenness of the paved surface, set a straight 2 × 4 on its narrow edge, across several stones, and look for gaps between the pavers and the 2 × 4. To check the pitch over several stones, place a level on top of the 2 × 4 or directly on the stones.

Outdoor Lighting

You're just as likely to use a patio or courtyard at night as you are during the day, so consider adding outdoor lighting, especially around areas that are difficult to negotiate in the dark. Lights set near the ground are much more appealing than glaring spotlights positioned in the eaves of a house. They're also much friendlier to creatures such as bats, lunar moths, and a host of nighttime pollinators.

Low-voltage outdoor lighting kits, for use with outdoor outlets, are available for do-it-yourselfers and are very easy to install. (If you don't have an outdoor outlet, consult with an electrician.) The lighting system for this project, which is shown in the photo on page 85, was easy to install and is basically maintenance-free.

Lay out the cable before you spread the gravel bed, placing it on the soil around the site's outer edge or beneath the area to be paved. After grading this project site, I ran the low-voltage cable from the house, across the paving site, and down an 8-inch-wide (20-cm) strip of planting-bed soil that I'd left between the existing timber retaining wall and the paving site. I then covered the short length of cable that crossed the paving site with gravel. After I completed the project, the property owners attached the lights to the exposed length of cable along the retaining wall and then buried that portion of the cable in the strip of soil.

The rock dust that fills these patio joints blends well with the colors of the pavers.
The 2 x 4 along one edge helps check the overall evenness of the stones.

Setting the Gravel and Filling the Joints

After laying out several stones, stand on them as you use your metal rod to set the gravel that's below the layer of finer material. (If you've added a layer of road bond between the gravel and rock dust or sand, skip this step.) Next, rather than filling the joints with gravel, as you might with fieldstone pavers, fill them with rock dust or coarse sand. Flagstone is too thin to stay stable when the joints are filled with gravel; finer materials are required to anchor these stones securely.

Soak the filled joints with water in order to settle the material into the gravel beneath. Repeat,

adding and soaking more rock dust or sand until the joints are filled to within ½ inch (13 mm) of the upper surfaces of the pavers. When the pavers have dried, sweep the remaining rock dust or sand into the joints.

Simple Stone Paths

The simplest kind of stone path consists of stone pavers set directly into the soil. You won't need fancy tools: just a shovel with a square blade, a mattock, a brick-

If your soil is firm and well drained, the easiest way to create a
stone path is to set fieldstone pavers directly into the soil.

and-block mason's hammer, and a wheelbarrow. You
will need firm, well-drained soil, as pavers placed
right into loam or very damp soil will sink. If your
soil is spongy, either place each stone on its own bed
of gravel or consider making the walkway project
shown on page 92 instead.

To make a simple stone path, first outline the site
with a garden hose, sprinkled corn meal, or string lines
and stakes. A comfortable path width is about 3 feet
(91 cm). You don't need to excavate the entire site; just
remove the sod.

Start by laying out a few pavers, arranging them in
any manner that pleases your eye. Unless the stones are
so far apart that someone might trip in the gaps between
them, the width of the joints isn't critical. The narrower
the joints, however, the less room there will be for
unwanted plants to grow.

To match the stones up without leaving large gaps
between them, you'll probably need to trim tapered edges
from a few. To fill any large gaps that are unavoidable, just
plug in smaller pavers, selecting stones that will reach deeply
enough into the soil to make them secure and stable.

The slight pitch of this stone path directs water away from a house.

Once you've arranged a few stones to your satisfaction, dig a hole for each one, flipping the stone back so you can reach the soil. Use a mattock or digging spade to rough-cut the hole; then refine its shape with the tapered blade of a brick-and-block mason's hammer. To compensate for settling, the upper surface of each stone should rise just above ground level. (If your soil isn't firm enough to support the stones, add a bed of gravel to each excavated hole.)

Test-fit each paver in its hole. If the paver's height isn't correct, add or remove soil to raise or lower it.

Tamp any added soil down thoroughly (a rubber mallet works well here) before replacing the stone. Use a level to make sure the upper surfaces of the pavers you've set are even. When the stones are at the correct height, fill the joints around them with soil. To stabilize the stones, use your rubber mallet or the blunt end of one of your hammer handles to pack the added soil firmly around the edges. Continue setting stones in this fashion until your path is finished.

Because simple stone paths don't usually have borders, surrounding vegetation will gradually creep into the joints between the pavers. Either trim these invaders while they're small (if you leave them unchecked, they'll eventually cover the pavers) or fill the joints with plants you've selected and set out yourself.

Stepping-Stone Paths

The easiest way to lay a stepping-stone path (a method that works best in firm, well-drained soil) is to set large stones directly into the ground. (See "Simple Stone Paths" for instructions.) Arrange the stepping stones as you like, but take care to place them so that stepping from one to another is comfortable and safe. Once the stones are in place, pack soil firmly around each one.

The stepping stones shown in the photo at the bottom of this page were set on a base of rock dust, which was spread on top of clay soil. To make a similar path, dig a trench a little wider than the largest stone and spread a 2-inch-thick (5-cm) bed of rock dust in it. Lay out the stones, fill the empty portions of the trench with rock dust, and tamp the rock dust down firmly.

In poorly-drained soil, stepping stones should be set on a gravel bed in an excavated trench and then packed with rock dust or gravel.

Garden beds are made more accessible by a simple stone path.

The bed of rock dust under and around these stepping stones stabilizes them. The steel edging material shown in the foreground defines one edge of a wide footpath.

Stone Walkways

This walkway design works well in a variety of situations. Its timber borders serve as an attractive visual accent and prevent the surrounding lawn from invading the joints between the rough-quarried stones.

This project is dry-laid in much the same way as the paving projects described earlier in this chapter. The instructions that follow will also work with other paving and border materials, although you'll need to make one important adaptation if you use flagstone or other types of pavers (see page 81).

The walkway shown in this photo is set on well-drained soil, so the site isn't pitched. If your site isn't well drained, refer to the section "Improving Drainage" on page 94 before preparing the site.

This project was built by my friend Sammy Cox, who decided to replace the deteriorating concrete path to his front door with a more welcoming walkway.

Selecting a Border Material

Squared timbers (4 × 4s, 6 × 6s, and 8 × 8s) are among the most common border materials for walkways, but 4 × 6 and 6 × 8 lumber will also work. Large timbers will last longer than smaller ones, and pressure-treated timbers will last the longest. If you don't want to use treated lumber, select a dense, long-lasting hardwood instead. Hardwood lasts longer than untreated softwood, especially if it's set on a gravel bed, and in time, hardwood also weathers to a beautiful, natural color. Unfortunately, hardwood timbers are sometimes difficult to find. To locate nearby sources, search online for "Sawmills" or "Lumber."

Using lumber of any kind will restrict you to straight-lined walkway designs. To create turns in the walkway, use a chain saw or circular saw to make angled end cuts where timber ends meet. For a more rustic look, use hardwood logs or flat stones set on their edges.

Preparing the Site

You don't need to pitch a walkway site on well-drained soil, but the site shouldn't slope down toward your home or any other structure. Sketch your design on paper first. Then use string lines and stakes set low to the ground to lay out the design at your site.

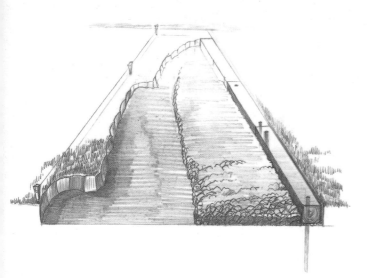

Excavated walkway trench with gravel bed and timbers.

Before you begin, refer to the walkway illustration above, which shows two different stages of walkway construction: the excavation of the trench (left) and the placement of the timber borders and gravel bed (right).

Lay out the timbers just inside the string lines and make end cuts as required to create any angled turns. When you're satisfied with the border layout, set the timbers off to the sides of the site. Remove any sod and other vegetation within the string lines.

Depending on the sizes of your timbers and stones, you'll probably have to excavate your trench to two different depths. The portion of the trench directly beneath the paving stones must be deep enough to hold a 4-inch-thick (10 cm) gravel bed and the paving stones set on that bed. The timbers, however, must be set on a shallower, 2-inch-deep (5 cm) gravel bed, and their upper surfaces must be kept just above ground level.

To estimate the required depth of the trench beneath the pavers, add 4 inches to the average thickness of your paving stones. To estimate the depth of the trench beneath the squared timbers, add 2 inches (5 cm) to the timber thickness. In most cases, the trench will be deeper beneath the paving stones than it is beneath the timbers.

The next step is to excavate the site. As you dig the trench, if you notice any wet, spongy spots in the soil, pack them firmly with large pieces of gravel or small rubble stones.

Spread out the gravel in the trench. Make sure that the bed is at least 4 inches (10 cm) deep down the center of the trench and 2 inches (5 cm) deep along the edges, where the timbers will be set.

Installing the Timber Border

In each timber, drill a series of ½-inch-diameter (13 mm) holes, spacing them 2 to 3 feet (61 to 91 cm) apart. Next, set two timbers on their gravel beds, opposite to one another and just inside the string lines. Adjust them on top of the gravel so that their upper surfaces are slightly above ground level. If you have a 4-foot-long (1.2 m) level, place it across the timbers to make sure their upper surfaces are even. (If your level is too short to span the gap between the timbers, set a length of 2 × 4 across them and place the level on the 2 × 4.) Repeat these steps to position the other timbers.

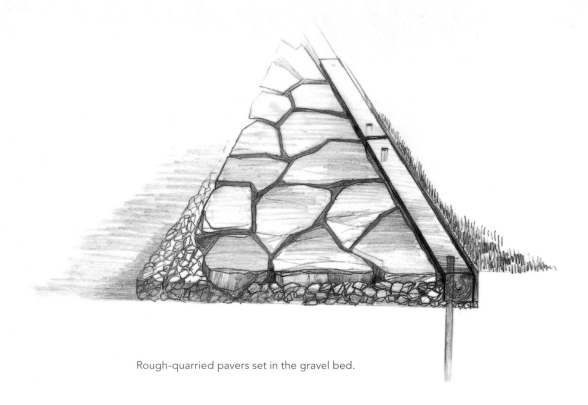

Rough-quarried pavers set in the gravel bed.

To anchor the timbers in place, drive 2-foot-long (61-cm) sections of rebar through the holes. The rebar sections should rest flush with the upper surfaces of the timbers or, if you plan to plug the holes with wood plugs, slightly below them.

Improving Drainage

In poorly-drained soils, it's wise to pitch the portion of the trench directly beneath the paving stones so that water will run down the length of the trench and discharge at the low end. A perforated drainage pipe, positioned in the center of the trench and running down its length, will also help. To prepare the trench for a pipe, dig both sides so they slope down toward the center;

these sloped surfaces will help direct water into the perforated pipe. Wrap the pipe in landscape fabric, position it in the trench, and spread the gravel bed over it.

To help correct poor drainage in spongy soils, add a 2-inch-thick (5-cm) bed of packed road bond to the bottom of the pitched trench. The layer of road bond will shed water, while the pitch of the trench will direct the water away from the site.

If your site just can't be pitched and soil drainage is poor, build the walkway above ground instead of setting it at ground level. Use timbers that are 6 to 8 inches (15 to 20 cm) thick, placing them on 2-inch-thick (5-cm) gravel beds just inside the string lines. Then spread a 2- to 4-inch-thick (5- to 10-cm) gravel bed for the pavers right on top of the sod-stripped soil between the timbers. Timber borders placed above ground level tend to look a little stark. Planting dense ground covers and bedding plants along their outer edges will help soften their appearance.

Setting the Pavers

Before setting the pavers, refer to the illustration to the left. Then review the paving instructions for the "Field-stone Entryway and Courtyard" on pages 72–93. You'll set these rough-quarried stones in much the same way. If you choose to use thinner pavers (including flagstone or brick), you must spread a 2-inch-thick (5 cm) bed of coarse sand or rock dust on top of the gravel bed before setting the stones. Although thick stones will be stable when they're set on a gravel bed, thinner stones require a layer of finer material to make them stable.

Start at one end of the walkway, selecting and laying out pavers on the gravel bed and making sure their upper surfaces are even with those of the timbers. Leave 1-inch-wide (2.5 cm) joints between the stones.

After you've laid out all the stones, use gravel (or, if you're working with thin pavers, rock dust or coarse sand) to adjust their heights. Remember that a pry bar or crowbar is the tool of choice for lifting stones. If a stone seems a bit high at one end, either remove gravel from beneath it or stamp on it to settle it.

Using your gravel-setting tool, set the stones as usual, adding gravel (or finer material) when necessary to fill any voids beneath them. To fill the joints, add gravel, rock dust, or sand.

Design Techniques

By all means experiment with your walkway's surface design. Rather than setting the stones section by section, for example, try laying out large stones in groups of two or three, along the entire walkway, matching the stone edges in each group. Then connect the groups of large stones by filling in with medium-sized and small stones. (When you're creating a narrow paving project such as a walkway, setting the pavers after laying all of them out is easy because you can work from both sides.)

To help water move off paths, many masons "crown" the paving by pitching the stones to slope from the center of the path down towards both edges. The very slight pitch of the stones produces a barely perceptible arc in the center of the path. When crowning a narrow path, be sure to use small stones, as pitching large ones in a limited space is almost impossible.

CHAPTER FIVE

MORTARED STONEWORK

In the first few chapters of this book, you've learned about different types of stone, the tools used in stonemasonry, and building techniques for dry-laid stonework. This chapter on mortared stonework will open up new possibilities and many interesting options for using stone in the landscape, on the exterior of your house, and even inside your home. For those who are dedicated dry-stone enthusiasts, and others who may feel a bit intimidated by even the slightest mention of mortar, I hope this section will spark your interest, allay your fears, and empower you to give it a try.

This cozy backyard includes a paved patio, a mortared bench wall, a fire ring, and dry-laid steps.

Basics and Techniques

So why bother using mortar to set stone? Isn't it diffi-cult? Honestly, I don't find mortared stonework any more difficult than dry-laid, though you do have to factor in mixing and using mortar, which admittedly can be a bit mysterious at first. There's no doubt that mortared stonework is different from dry-laid work, yet the two methods employ many similar techniques. One is not really better than the other; each has its place. For particular projects, mortared stonework is recommended, and sometimes required, such as stacking a stone veneer against a block retaining wall, using flag-stone paving on a concrete pad for a patio or walkway, or for building a hearth and fireplace, to mention a few.

This section isn't a complete catalog of everything you can accomplish with mortar and stone, but rather an in-depth look at the techniques used for setting stone in mortar, along with all the basic information you'll need for setting up your project site.

A large concrete pad serves as a base for the patio, the fire circle, and the wall.

Concrete Footings and Pads

The biggest difference between dry-laid and mortared stonework is that mortared stonework is rigid and doesn't allow for the slightest bit of movement between stones. For this reason, a solid, concrete foundation is required in most mortared stoneworking projects (as well as in other masonry applications, such as brick and block work). A concrete foundation gives complete, unyielding support that's essential to maintain the integrity of the project. Vertical stonework, such as a veneered concrete block wall, requires footings (trenches) dug in the ground, that serve as a form for which to pour concrete. Concrete pads are created for mortared horizontal stonework such as a flagstone patio. It's the footings and pads that account for a bulk of the extra time and expense involved in mortared work.

There are some situations where concrete footings or pads won't be necessary. You won't need them in locations where the ground doesn't freeze. Also, if your project is relatively small, such as a 12- to 18-inch-high (30.5 to 45.7 cm) border wall, you could get away with a packed gravel footing. In all other situations, mortared stonework without a concrete foundation is likely to settle irregularly and be influenced by frost heave, which causes the mortar to crack, weakening the stonework and causing water damage and further deterioration. Many situations involving a concrete footing or pad will require the approval of your local building inspector, especially if you live in a city or suburban setting. This usually happens after the footers are dug or the formwork is set for a concrete pad and before the concrete is poured.

Concrete

Concrete is a thick, fluid mixture made up of gravel, sand, portland cement, and water. It's poured into footings that have been dug 1 to 3 feet (0.3 to 0.9 m) below the ground's surface, depending on the frost line at a particular site. A concrete pad is poured onto a base of crushed stone and contained by constructed wooden forms. When the concrete sets up (cures), it provides a strong and uniform foundation on which to build.

Estimating Amounts of Concrete for a Pad

The easiest and sometimes most efficient way to pour concrete is to order ready-mix that's delivered in a concrete truck. Generally, the smallest amount a concrete supplier will deliver is 1 yard (0.9 m). To calculate the square footage of a square or rectangular pad, measure the length times the width in feet and the thickness in a fraction of a foot. In most cases, a concrete pad will be 4 inches (10.2 cm) thick, which is one-third of a foot (0.33). If you're dealing with more organic shapes, measure as though you were working with a square or rectangle. This will give you a liberal amount of square footage, which can then be rounded off to a more

conservative number before dividing by 27 to get the cubic yardage. (There are 27 cubic feet in a cubic yard, and 1 cubic yard equals 0.5 cubic meters.)

For example, if your patio is 12 feet (3.6 m) wide and 20 feet (6 m) long, those two figures multiplied together give you 240 square feet (22 m²) of surface area. Multiply 240 by 0.33 and you get approximately 80 cubic feet (2.3 m³), which equals approximately 3 cubic yards of concrete (divide 80 by 27).

Estimating Amounts of Concrete for a Footing

Concrete footings need to be poured a minimum of 8 inches (20.3 cm) thick or two-thirds of a foot (0.67). To measure amounts of concrete for footings, multiply the length by the width by 0.67, and follow the instructions above.

For example, a footer 2 feet (0.6 m) wide multiplied by its length of 20 feet (6 m), gives you 40 square feet (3.6 m²). Multiply 40 by 0.67 to get 26.8 cubic feet (0.8 m³). Divide 26.8 by 27 to convert cubic feet to cubic yards. You'll need approximately 1 yard (0.9 m) of concrete.

Pouring Concrete

If the concrete truck can't be positioned close to where the concrete will be poured, you have the option of moving it from the truck in a wheelbarrow. I strongly suggest having at least two wheelbarrows and three people available for pouring more than 1 yard (0.9 m) of concrete.

Have your site completely ready for when the truck arrives. Plan a route for getting the truck right up to the project or as close as possible. The formwork and footings should be ready to receive the concrete before the truck arrives. Formwork is discussed in the projects' instructions.

A freestanding, solid-stone wall separates a kitchen and family room. Granite cubes line the arched pass-through, and large slabs of stone strengthen the stonework and function as shelves.

Tools such as shovels, steel tooth rakes, trowels, striking boards, wooden floats, gloves, and rubber boots should be close at hand. Wet the site down in advance the day before if the weather has been dry. Concrete needs to cure slowly, and excessively dry sites will pull moisture out of the mix too quickly.

There's a limit to how much time you'll have when pouring concrete; things happen quickly once the concrete truck arrives. As the concrete is being poured for a slab, use shovels and steel-toothed rakes to spread it around. Once the form is topped off, you'll need to strike the concrete with a long 2 × 4 that's longer than the width of your form. Striking will knock down the high spots and even the surface out level with the top of your form.

To strike the pad, with the help of a partner, stretch the 2 × 4 along the top edge of the form. With short strokes, run the 2 × 4 from one end of the pad to the other, tapping or shimmying it along the form as you go. The vibrations created by the tapping help the concrete settle. At the same time, the 2 × 4 is helping you level the concrete as you move it across the form. At this point, you may have to add or remove concrete to achieve an even surface.

Immediately after striking the surfaces smooth it with a bull or darby float. Then trowel the surface of the concrete. In this case, you'll be covering over the concrete with stone, so the finished concrete surface doesn't have to be perfectly smooth. Trowel the edges first, and as the concrete hardens, use pieces of plywood to kneel on as you work out into the center. Continue smoothing the surface until there's no water left.

Concrete footings and pads should cure a minimum of 24 hours before working on top of them. In extremely hot, dry weather, wet the surface of a concrete pad with a hose every two hours during the day once it has set up firm.

Mixing Your Own Concrete

You can also mix your own concrete at the site, especially if you're working on a small patio or a short length of wall. Buy premixed concrete that comes in 40-, 60-, or 80-pound (18.2-, 27.2-, or 36.3-kg) bags. Read the specifics for the different types of premixed concrete: some are for footers that are load bearing, while others are "quick setting" and considerably more expensive. All you have to do is add water and mix with a mortar hoe in a wheelbarrow. Read the specific instructions on the bag. These premixed bags are certainly convenient and cost-effective for small jobs.

I've found that the standard concrete recipe works best with the projects in this book:
  – 1 part portland cement (type I)★
  – 3 parts clean builder's sand★★
  – 4 parts gravel (crushed, washed stone from ¼ to 1 inch [6 mm to 2.5 cm])
  – Water, clean enough to drink

The amount of water added to a batch of mortar will vary depending upon the sand's dampness. Once you've mixed a batch, you'll have a general idea of approximately how much water to add. Remember to add very small increments of water until the mix has the consistency of oatmeal.

★Portland cement (type I) comes in 47- and 94-pound (21.3- and 42.7-kg) bags.

★★Builders sand is available at most building supply businesses and concrete-block plants. This sand is sharp edged and finely graded. Always keep your sandpile completely covered with a tarp or large sheet of plastic when you're not working. Covering the sand pile will keep the sand dry and clean. Extremely wet sand is much harder to mix consistently with the other dry ingredients when mixing manually with a mortar hoe.

Start a batch by thoroughly mixing the sand and cement together using a mortar hoe, then work in enough water to make a thick, soupy mix. Add several shovels of gravel, mixing it in with the mortar hoe, then add several more, and mix. Continue until all the gravel is added. If the mixture gets too stiff to mix, add more water. It's best to use the concrete soon after the mixing is completed.

Mortar

Mortar makes up about 10 to 20 percent of the total volume in a stone wall. Its function is to bond the stone and other masonry fasteners together. Mortar is similar to concrete, but it doesn't contain gravel and its consistency is quite different. Also, mason's lime is added to mortar to create a rich, sticky mixture. The material that brick and block masons use is quite porous, so the mortar they use is very wet, almost runny. Most stone worth using will be less porous than brick or block, so for the two styles of stonework described in this chapter, the mortar will be much stiffer.

For only one or two novice masons working on a mortared stone paving project, a wheelbarrow will do for mixing mortar. To keep your pile of sand clean, keep it covered.

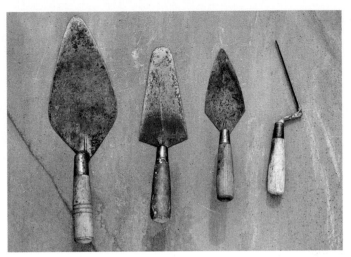

From left to right: a brick mason's trowel, a duckbill trowel, a pointing trowel, and a slicker trowel

Tools for Mortaring

A *mortar pan* or *wheelbarrow* is sufficient to mix mortar in for small jobs. I tend to work directly out of these, depending on how close I can get them to the stonework. If the stonework goes taller than 5 feet (1.5 m), and I start working on walk board and scaffolding, I use 5-gallon (19 L) buckets.

Two *mortar hoes* make the mixing go faster. A smaller mortar hoe with a 7 inch (17.8 cm) blade and two holes in it is easy to use. A larger hoe requires more strength to pull and is awkward to use if two people are mixing mortar together in a wheelbarrow.

A *square shovel* works best for shoveling sand and mortar mix and for scooping wet mortar out of the mixing pan.

I prefer a *medium-sized trowel* for placing mortar while setting stone, because it's easier to work the mortar in around the backside of the stonework. A *small buttering trowel* is handy for working mortar into tight spaces. If I need to place a large amount of mortar behind the stonework, I use a *shovel*.

Mortar Mixes

As with concrete, premixed mortar is available and can be considered cost-effective for smaller jobs.

The standard mix for creating your own mortar is:
- 1 part portland cement (type I)
- 1 part masonry cement (type S)
  6 parts sand★
- Water

★ You want sand particles that are coarse with sharp edges. For this reason, avoid using beach sand or play sand (meant for sandboxes). Both of these have rounded edges. River sand is fine if you can find it.

Masonry Cement

There are many masonry cements available. Choose the cement that will fit your needs best, which in this case is type S. The exact ingredients and proportions in masonry cements usually are proprietary information.

Type M mortar is a durable mortar with high strength that's best used in foundations, stone veneer, and retaining walls. It can handle high compression loads.

It's in the Bag

At the building supply store, it's common for an employee to load bags of cement for you. Give him or her a hand if possible. Once you get a tear in a bag, it can be a mess, so if there's cement spilling out, refuse the bag. Also, only buy bags of cement mix from businesses that keep them in a covered, dry space. The bags should be somewhat pliable, so if you get a bag that's as hard as a rock that means it has gotten wet, set up, and is of no use. Even the moisture in the air can cause the bags to harden somewhat. For this reason, I hold off until all my other materials are on site before purchasing the cement mixture I need. Once the material is on site, it should be kept off the ground and completely covered with plastic.

Type S mortar has the ability to give when under pressure. It's good for stonework that will be subjected to normal compression loads. It has good adhesion, making this a good mortar for vertical veneer work and setting paving stones to a concrete pad.

Type N mortar is a general-purpose mortar for structures above grade such as masonry veneers and interior walls.

Type O mortar is for non-load bearing walls and exterior veneers that won't freeze if they get wet.

Portland cement-lime mortar is a durable mortar with a consistent hardening rate and a high compressive strength. The lime adds workability, water retention, and elasticity.

Mixing Mortar Manually

For most small projects, mixing mortar by hand is much more practical than renting a mortar mixer. A 6-cubic-foot (0.18 m³) wheelbarrow is fairly inexpensive and easy to mix mortar in. Mortar pans come in several sizes. A small one 2½ × 5 feet (0.8 × 1.5 m) will hold 6 cubic feet (0.18 m³) of mortar and is a convenient size. Set the mortar pan close to the sandpile or near your building site. I usually set the pan up with a concrete block underneath each corner to reduce some of the bending when mixing.

Regardless of what method you choose for mixing the mortar, it's best to keep your sand and mortar mix materials in the same location, preferably close to a source of water. Be sure to cover the materials with a tarp when you stop work for the day.

To start a batch of mortar, shovel in the sand first. Then add the other ingredients specific to your mix. Use a mortar hoe to dry-mix the ingredients until you get a uniform color. Pull the dry mix to one end of the mixing pan, and add 1 gallon (3.8 l) of water at the opposite end. Using the hoe, begin pulling sections of the dry mix into the water, mixing the two with a chopping action. Pull the wet mortar to the opposite end of the dry mix, add more water, and repeat the process until all the dry mix is wet. If more water is necessary, add it in small increments, because it's easy to add too much water and end up with a soupy mix.

There's no set formula for just how much water to add to a particular batch. The dampness of the sand, the desired composition, the absorption rate of the materials, and the weather conditions all have to be taken into consideration. I suggest setting aside a couple of gallons of the dry mix from your first batch just in case a batch becomes too wet.

Continue mixing the mortar with a chopping action to thoroughly mix in the water. Pockets of the dry mix tend to accumulate in the corners and on the very bottom of the mixing pan. Check these areas with the hoe. You may have to repeat the process of chopping and pulling the mortar two or three times to completely mix a batch.

Mortar Consistency

The mortar used in the dry-stack look is mixed drier than other mortars. It should be slightly sticky, yet still crumbly. Take a handful and pat it into a ball. It should hold together easily. Drop it a couple of feet from one hand to the other. The ball should crumble and fall apart on impact. If you're working in dry, hot weather, the mortar should be mixed slightly wetter, but it should not be soupy.

When stacking stone with a visible mortar joint or laying mortared paving, the mortar should be as wet as possible without being runny. Mortar of this consistency can be spread easily with a trowel. Consistency of ingredients from one batch to the next is important.

Gas and Electric Mortar Mixers

Mortar mixers will save time and physical labor, and I recommend one for larger jobs. A small, 4-cubic-foot (0.12 m³) mixer will do if you're working alone. If two or more masons are laying stone, a 6-cubic-foot (0.18 m³) mixer is needed. Be aware that a mortar mixer is used only to mix mortar and not concrete.

Set the mortar mixer up on blocks to allow the mortar to dump directly into the wheelbarrow.

Mortar mixers can be rented on a daily, weekly, or monthly basis. You'll need a vehicle set up for towing in order to haul the mixer to the job site. If you're not familiar with running a mortar mixer, someone at the rental business will explain how to operate it.

Working with Mortar

There are three stages of the mortar's curing process. Work you have just completed is *new* or *fresh*. The next day, it's at the *green stage*. When the work is stable, the final stage is *cured*, which happens four to six days later.

If you're working on a 10-foot (3-m) stone wall, you'll be able to lay only several courses before having to take a break. When stonework is in the fresh stage, it's subject to movement, because the mortar hasn't bonded with the stones or set up enough to handle much weight. Rushing the work at this point can cause the stonework to bow outward. Once it's in the green stage, the stonework is a lot more stable, and it won't have any movement at all. Finally, after several days, the mortar will be cured.

The recessed mortar in this wall turns the joints into shadow lines, putting more emphasis on the stones' shapes and textures.

Veneer

Veneered stone facing is a facade used to mask concrete or frame-structured walls. The majority of stonework in new home construction is veneered rather than cost-prohibitive solid stone. With a few tools, some mortar, and stone, you'll be able to veneer the exterior of a foundation wall, a concrete block fence, or even an interior wall.

There are different styles of mortared stonework, each influenced by the type, size, and shape of stone used, as well as by how tightly the stones are fit together and by the pattern used. The two main styles are dry-stacked, which is a mortared wall that looks like a dry-stacked wall, and the visible-joint style. Instructions for both styles are included in this section.

Veneering is especially trouble free if the completed project is less than 5 feet (1.5 m) tall. Any taller than that, and you'll need to start using scaffolding or at least a walk board on top of concrete blocks. Also, before beginning, make sure the wall you're about to veneer is fairly plumb.

Dry-Stack-Look Veneer

This type of stonework has the look of a true dry-stacked stone wall, and you'll use similar building techniques for setting the stones. With the dry-stack look, stones are set using a stiff mortar that's placed between the wall you're veneering and around the back of the stones. With a 6- to 8-inch-thick (15.2- and 20.3-cm) veneer, there's enough depth to stack each course of stone for a dry fit before setting them in mortar. This style of stonework is great for facing concrete foundation walls, block retaining walls, freestanding walls, and interior walls for sunrooms and greenhouse additions (stone provides extra thermal mass).

Considerations

As discussed on page 99, footings evenly distribute the weight of the stonework and safeguard against settling and frost heave. The required thickness for a concrete footing is 8 inches (20.3 cm). If you have a trench that's 2 to 3 feet (0.6 to 0.9 m) deep (because of your frost line), that leaves a lot of space to fill in order to start your stone wall. One option is to lay courses of block on top of the concrete until you've reached the top of the trench. Another option is to fill the entire trench with concrete, which is not that much more expensive.

After the block- or wood-constructed wall is built, you'll need a minimum surface area of 8 inches (20.3 cm) left on the footing to set the stonework.

Wall Ties

With a mortared stone veneer, metal wall ties are used as extra assurance to secure the stonework to the wall being veneered. Wall ties are thin, galvanized metal strips, 7 inches (17.8 cm) long and roughly 1 inch (2.5 cm) wide. With a concrete block wall, the wall ties should be set in the mortar joints when the block wall is

Metal wall tie.

A mortared stone veneer requires a good selection of workable stone and some patience. This wall sits on top of a sunroom's concrete pad, and concrete block steps are veneered with the same stone.

The wall ties should be attached to the wall before you begin stacking your veneer.

This mortared stone veneer covers a wood-sheathed wall with a layer of roofing felt, metal stucco lath, and wall ties.

laid or with concrete screws if they're set after the block wall has been built. There are two holes in wall ties for attaching them to the necessary length using one nail or screw. With a wood-frame wall, use one nail (8 penny) to attach each tie to the wood sheathing, preferably in line with the wall studs. Place wall ties roughly every 16 inches (40.6 cm), horizontally and vertically (figure 1).

Optional Materials

Stucco lath is a panel of metal mesh with a honeycomb pattern. It comes in $2\frac{1}{2} \times 8$-foot (0.75×2.4-m) sheets and can be used in addition to wall ties over a wood-constructed wall. They're hung by setting 1-inch (2.5-cm) nails around the perimeter and down the center. Another option for exterior wood-constructed walls that will be veneered is to use roofing felt as a vapor barrier to cover the sheathing.

Selecting Stone

For tight-fitting stonework, shape your stone as needed. With stones laid along their bedding plane, two flat surfaces are best with at least one good face to show in the wall. Stones stood on their narrow edge may need to be trimmed to produce a surface even enough so it can stand on the course below it. Do all of your trimming off the wall.

If you're not satisfied with the color of a particular stone, it's fine to combine two or more types of stone with different colors. If you do this though, you'll need to mix them evenly to achieve a pleasing blend of color.

How Much Stone You'll Need

See pages 56–57 for details.

Site Setup

In order to keep the stonework plumb, you'll set the face of each stone 8 inches (20.3 cm) from the wall you're veneering. Choosing a depth (wall thickness) of at least 8 inches (20.3 cm) will give you plenty of options of stone from which to choose. Measure and mark from the face of the block wall to the face of each stone you're setting with a gauge stick or a measuring tape. This will also produce a veneer with an even surface.

Preparing the Foundation

In order to lay the dry-stack look for a foundation wall, you'll need a minimum of 6 inches (15.2 cm) of exposed footing to set the stone on, and 8 inches (20.3 cm) is preferable with an 8-inch-thick (20.3-cm) veneer. I've found it common practice in new home construction for only 4 inches (10.2 cm) to be left on the concrete footing after the block foundation is laid. If you want an 8-inch (20.3-cm) veneer, you'll need to express this point to the builder and architect before the home's foundation is laid.

Dry-Fitting the Stones

After you've prepared your site and attached wall ties and/or stucco laths, you can begin dry-fitting your first course. Dry-fitting the stones with each course allows you to concentrate on getting them to fit just the way you want before they're set in mortar. Read the section on building a dry-laid stone retaining wall on pages 60–61 for more information.

Set your cornerstones and wall ends first, and then fill-in between, the way you would with a dry-stone wall. If you're working on a wall more than 20 feet (6 m) long, you may want to dry-fit 10 feet (3 m) of a course at a time and then set that part of the course in mortar. This will allow the first 10 feet (3 m) to begin

Figure 1 Wall ties are worked in between the courses of stonework.

setting up while you dry-fit the rest of the course. One important consideration is to make sure the wall ties you've secured to the wall line up with the courses as you lay them. You'll be bending the ties into the joints as you add your mortar.

Dry-set stones should have a gravity fit. This means they should stay where you've placed them until you're ready to mortar them into place. This may involve shimming a stone from behind or placing a small, temporary wedge underneath the front edge to hold some stones in place. Combining small, medium, and large stones from one course to the next will make a more pleasing composition.

When laying the stones, avoid placing them with their upper surfaces pitched out toward the wall's face. Stones set this way may slip out of the wall someday. The mortar set at the back of the stonework can be used in the final adjustment of a stone's angle.

Weep Holes

When veneering a concrete block retaining wall, you'll need to add weep holes that allow water that will accumulate behind the wall to pass through it. As the concrete block wall is being built, place 16-inch (40.6-cm) lengths of 2-inch-diameter (5.1-cm) plastic pipe every 4 feet (1.2 m) between the first course of concrete block. Set the pipes 4 inches (10.2 cm) above the foundation's height, extending from the back edge of the block out to where it will be worked into the stone veneer.

Corners and Wall Ends

Cornerstones will have two faces that meet at a 90-degree angle. Stones with approximate 90-degree corners can be alternated with true 90-degree cornerstones. Set your cornerstones at the wall ends first from one course to the next and then set the stones between them. Taller cornerstones may serve for more than one course of stonework before another is set.

Shiners

Stones stood on their narrow edge and revealing a large face in the stonework are called *shiners*. Shiners can be as thin as 3 inches (7.6 cm) or as thick as the depth of the veneer (6 to 8 inches [15.2 to 20.3 cm]). Shiners mixed into your veneer break up the pattern and play off the smaller faces to create an interesting look. They're also a great way to take up space. Special attention needs to be paid to these stones while setting them and in building up the stonework around them.

Mortaring the Stones

If you're veneering a concrete block wall, spray the section you're about to veneer with a hose until it's thoroughly soaked. This will prevent the concrete from sucking moisture out of the mortar. After dry-fitting a portion of the first course, you're ready to set the stones in mortar. Remove several of the stones you've just dry-fit (remembering their order) and spread a 1-inch-thick by 6-inch-wide (2.5 by 15.2 cm) band of mortar at the base of the wall. Set the first cornerstone and proceed with setting the rest of the course.

Mortar Recipe

(follow the mixing instructions on pages 104–105). The mortar recipe for this type of stonework is:

1 part portland cement (type I)

1 part type 'S' masonry cement

6 parts sand

Water

Securing the Stones

To secure a stone in the mortar, push it down or lightly tap it with a hammer. Fill in around the back of the stones with mortar, mixing in rock chips in the larger voids. The backfill should be filled flush with the back edge of each stone's upper surface. Pack the mortar into place around the stones using the end of your trowel's handle or a stick of wood about the same diameter. You can also use your hand to pack the mortar. I usually wear a rubber glove on one hand to do this. The lime in mortar is caustic, and prolonged exposure will pull out the natural oils in your skin. Rinse your hands often and use moisturizing lotion at the end of the day.

To keep from constantly having to reach into the wheelbarrow or mortar pan, place one or two shovels of mortar on top of the veneer already set, slightly ahead of the stones you're about to set. A bucket of mortar by your side is also handy. At the end of each working session, leave the mortared backfill well below the top of the last stones you've worked on. When work resumes,

Located in Linville, North Carolina, this fieldstone veneer is backed up by a concrete block retaining wall that sits on a 2-foot-deep (61-cm) concrete foundation.

you'll fill the space you left during the previous work session with mortar and then continue backfilling. This allows the two mortar sessions to bond better.

As you're working with the mortar, keep it set back from the face of the stonework. Use the drier mortar I've described to work in areas directly behind each stone. I usually have a separate batch of slightly wetter mortar that's easier to work in between the stone's back edges and the block wall. If mortar works its way to the front of the stonework and fills in the joints, leave it to be raked out later.

Raking the Joints

Once the mortar has set for three hours or so, but hasn't completely hardened, rake back any visible mortar in the joints at least 1 inch (2.5 cm) with a narrow trowel or a

The cornerstones frame this impressive veneer.

stick. Under normal conditions, after four hours, the mortar will have hardened enough to make it difficult to rake it out. If you rake the joints back too soon, you'll notice the mortar will tend to smear. If this happens, wait awhile. Raking the joints is something you have to keep up with throughout a working session. After raking the joints, use a stiff-bristled brush to knock any mortar off the stonework's face.

Hardened and Cured Mortar

The mortar needs to cure slowly to fully bond with the stone. In extremely, hot, dry, windy weather, the mortar set in a wall can dry too fast, causing it to weaken considerably. To keep the mortared stonework from drying too quickly, spray the stonework with a fine mist when the mortar is hard enough not to run or wash out. Then cover the areas you're not working on with plastic sheeting or tarps. At the end of the day, mist the wall again and cover your work. Keep the work dampened and covered for at least a couple of days.

The Next Courses

Continue mortaring all the stones you have dry-fitted until a course is finished. Insert stone chips in the joint below to temporarily support a stone if it feels as if it'll lean out. If you're working with a fairly stiff mortar, you should be able to start your next course immediately. Dry-fit your next course of stone. If you have a number of small faces that create a series of joints close together, select a stretcher stone with a long face to fit over them. When a stone is mortared into place, it should feel secure and not move or rock in any direction.

Figure 2 A bond stone ties the narrow shiner into the stonework. Wall ties help secure the veneer to the wall.

Adding Shiners

To provide a secure surface on which to lay a shiner, you'll need to let the stonework's mortar set several hours. The bottom edge of a shiner should have good contact with the top edges of the stones on which it's sitting. Stand the stone up plumb so its face is in line with the face of the veneer (figure 2). To keep from constantly having to hold the stone in place, wedge a piece of scrap lumber between its top edge and the block wall. I usually set large shiners ½ inch (1.3 cm) back from the wall's face. This provides better contact with the stones that will surround it.

With the stone stood in place, you'll have a large void behind the stone to fill. Carefully work in some mortar behind the stone at its base. Then set the stones to either side of the shiner and continue to backfill behind it using small stones and rock chips mixed in with the mortar. Continue setting the courses of stone, making sure that the stones in contact with the shiner have a tight fit with its edges. When the rest of the stonework is even with the top of the shiner, remove the scrap piece of lumber and set a bond stone across the top of the shiner to tie the stonework back into the full depth of the veneer.

Bond stones span well into the depth or thickness of a wall and add strength to the wall by binding the stonework together. Use a bond stone directly above any narrow stone that only reaches back 3 to 4 inches (7.6 to 10.2 cm) into the veneer.

The Final Course

The final course of stone that meets up underneath capstones, the ceiling of an interior wall, or the siding on an exterior wall is a focal point. These stones should be shaped to fit the space they'll fill. Maintain the overall look of the stonework and avoid filling in this last space with a series of smaller stones.

Mortared Veneer Stonework with Visible Joints

Stonework with a visible joint will allow you to use stones that are rougher and more irregular in shape. A mortar joint ½ to ¾ inch (1.3 to 1.9 cm) is a good standard to work with, though 1-inch (2.5-cm) joints (or larger) are fine as long as you're as consistent as possible with the joint size throughout the wall. You'll follow the instructions for the dry-stack look veneer, with these exceptions:

This veneer with visible mortared joints uses a generous number of shiners:

This veneer covers a wood-sheathed wall with a layer of roofing felt, metal stucco lath, and wall ties. A string line is used to set the cornerstones. The exposed mortar joints have been raked back dramatically and will be finished later by the mason's helper.

- When you dry-fit the stones as described in the dry-stack look section, leave a ½-inch (1.3 cm) vertical gap between the stones in each course for the mortar.

- The mortar between each course should be set back about 1 inch (2.5 cm) from the stone's face and extend all the way back to the wall you're veneering. Setting the mortar back 1 inch (2.5 cm) will allow for some relief around the individual stones. Each stone should have a uniform mortar joint all the way around it.

- Since the exposed mortar joints are such a visual part of the wall, special attention needs to be given to them. Before the mortar has hardened, you'll need to strike the joints using a slicker trowel. Striking the joints gives them a uniform look and removes any gaps where the mortar meets the edges of the stones. If there are pockets or gaps in the joints, they'll need to be filled with mortar. Use the smaller pointing trowel or a narrow slicker trowel to pack the mortar into place. If the mortar extends out to the face of a stone or beyond, leave it until the mortar has set awhile and lost its watery sheen, then rake it back with a narrow, slicker trowel.

A stone hearth and fireplace surround are the focal points of this living room.

Veneering Inside the Home

Veneering an interior wall involves essentially the same processes as veneering an outside wall, but you need to make sure you have adequate support under the veneer, which means a concrete footing or pad. A proper footing or pad needs to be considered in the designing phase of your home's construction. Consult with a general contractor if veneering an interior wall is an afterthought to your home's original design.

The capstones on this low, freestanding mortared stone wall were pitched with a hammer and chisel and set to overhang slightly.

Freestanding Walls

There are two ways to build a freestanding, mortared stone wall. The first one is veneering both sides of a concrete block wall. The other is building a double-faced, solid stone wall. Both methods involve digging and pouring a footer for the walls to sit on.

Veneered Freestanding Wall

So why bother laying a block wall if you can build a solid stone wall in a similar way? The sole purpose of the block wall is to make it easier to lay the stone, and keep the wall plumb and even in thickness, using the blocks as a gauge. The block wall is a plumb, rigid surface from which to measure, so you end up with an even stone face on each side of the wall. To build a veneered freestanding wall, refer to the veneering instructions on pages 106–113 as well as the instructions for laying capstones on pages 67–68.

Both the dry-stack look and the visible mortar joint style will work for this project. You'll need a block wall laid with 4-, 6-, or 8-inch-wide (10.2-, 15.2-, or 20.3-cm) concrete blocks. These blocks are 8 inches (20.3 cm) tall and 16 inches (40.6 cm) in length. (Concrete blocks are actually 7⅝ inches [19.4 cm] tall, which accounts for a ⅜-inch [1-cm] mortar joint that's already figured into the overall measurement.) You'll have a 6- to 8-inch (15.2- to 20.3-cm) veneer on both sides of the block work, which means the stonework will make up 12 to 16 inches (30.5 to 40.6 cm) of the wall's overall thickness (figure 3). Consider how much thicker you want the wall to be and choose one of the three sizes of block listed above. Consult a blockmason or stonemason to help construct the initial block wall.

Figure 3 Beginning construction of a veneered freestanding wall

Footer Width

The width of your concrete footing should be 12 inches (30.5 cm) wider than the thickness of the wall, for walls up to 4 feet (1.2 m) tall. For walls taller than that, the foundation should be twice the width of the wall's thickness.

Design Considerations

If this is a low wall, 2 to 3 feet (0.6 to 0.9 m) tall, use the thinner, less imposing 4-inch (10.2-cm) blocks. On the other hand, if this is a perimeter wall that's in a large, open space, you may want to use the 8-inch (20.3 cm) blocks, which will make the wall thicker, giving it a more substantial look. For either the dry-stack look or the visible mortar joint style, follow the instructions described earlier in this section for laying the stone.

Mortar Recipe
(Follow the mixing instructions on pages 104–105.)
The mortar recipe for this type of stone work is:
2 parts portland cement (type I)
1 part type 'S' masonry cement
3 parts sand
Water

Other Considerations

- Remember to place wall ties in the block work every 16 inches (40.6 cm), both vertically and horizontally, as the concrete blocks are laid.

- The height of the block wall you're veneering is critical to the overall finished wall height. For this reason, you'll need to figure the number of courses of blocks necessary for the wall's height, while allowing room for the thickness of your capstones. For example, if you want the wall's finished height to be 3 feet (0.9 m), you'll need 4 courses of concrete blocks, which equals 32 inches (81.3 cm). That will leave you enough space to set capstones.

Freestanding Solid-Stone Wall

Low freestanding stone walls 3 feet (0.9 m) high are a beautiful way to separate your front yard from the neighborhood sidewalk or to border a patio. A taller freestanding wall, 4 to 5 feet (1.2 to 1.5 m) tall, is a substantial barrier, providing privacy and, if positioned properly, protection for plants and humans from harsh winds.

A solid-stone freestanding bench wall zig zags through the J. C. Raulston Garden in Raleigh, North Carolina.

This low, freestanding solid-stone wall was stacked without visible mortar joints. Wide bands of mortar spread across the joints in the top of the wall will keep moisture out.

To build a freestanding mortared wall, you'll incorporate many techniques that appear in other sections of this book. You'll follow the instructions for the freestanding dry-laid wall on pages 39–49, the instructions on footers and mortar that appear earlier in this section (pages 99–105), as well as the veneering instructions on pages 106–114. Along with these instructions, remember the following:

- For best results, mortar one layer at a time. In other words, you'll lay one course, and then lay the course on the opposite side before moving up to the next course.
- Use the mortar recipe on page 103.
- The middle of each course should be filled with mortar, pieces of rocks, and/or blocks and bricks.

A low, mortared stone retaining wall and mortared flagstone paving create an intimate spot to gather in the evening around a fire ring.

Paving

With this project you'll learn to work with flagstone and mortar to create a beautiful hardscape feature, such as a patio, landing, or walkway. Flagstone (flagging) is a general term used to describe stone used for paving. The crab orchard flagstone used in the project below is a medium to dense sandstone from eastern Tennessee. In this project, the flagstone is used as a veneer or overlay for a concrete pad.

Paving Your Site

You may decide to pave an open area or one that abuts a building's foundation wall. The instructions here will cover both scenarios. Your concrete pad will be the standard 4 inches (10.2 cm) thick, with a 1-inch (2.5-cm) bed of mortar and 1-inch-thick (2.5-cm) flagstone. This means the area you'll dig will be 6 inches (15.2 cm) deep. As with dry-laid paving, make sure the flagstone surface is at least 6 inches (15.2 cm) below any building siding.

Considerations

The simplest way to lay a flagstone surface is in a random pattern, with mortar joints averaging 1 inch (2.5 cm) in width. With this random pattern, you'll design as you go by simply setting the pieces in a manner that's pleasing to your eye, keeping in mind to mix the small, medium, and larger pieces, along with any odd colors, for an even and balanced-looking pattern. For a more controlled mortar-joint width and custom design, you'll need to cut and break away sections of most of the pieces of flagging, which takes time and effort (see Trimming Flagstone Pavers, page 84).

Selecting Stone

For a random placement design, use broken pieces of flagging instead of those with cut edges. Cut flagstone will work for this project but is considerably more expensive. Cut stone refers to flagging that's sawn into dimensional pieces, such as rectangles. Random pieces of flagging are sold by weight, while cut stone is priced by the square foot.

Pieces from ¾ to 3 inches (1.9 to 7.6 cm) thick work best. The flagstone you choose should have an even but gritty surface that offers good traction. A medium-density stone will hold up well under normal use around

Blue slate is a beautiful and durable paving material.

the home, while denser stone may be necessary if the project is in a public area where there's a considerable amount of foot traffic.

Delivering Flagstone

If you're lucky, the stone yard's delivery truck will have a boom on it that can mechanically remove the pallets at your site. Otherwise, the stone will have to be dumped or unloaded manually. If you plan on unloading the pieces by hand, you'll need to discuss this with the stone yard because of the extra time involved. Dumping thin flagstone on a hard surface can compromise its quality considerably. To absorb some of the shock to the stone in these situations, spread a layer of bark mulch at least 8 inches (20.3 cm) thick or stack several empty pallets exactly where the stone will land. Separate your stone into piles of large, medium, and small pieces. If the flagstones have soil caked on them, hose them off as you separate them.

How Much Stone You'll Need

If you're using a thin flagstone, 1 to 1½ inches (2.5 to 3.8 cm) thick, you'll get an average of 150 square feet (13.5 m²) per ton (0.9 t) of stone. With 3-inch-thick (7.6-cm) flagging, you'll be able to cover an area of approximately 75 square feet (6.8 m²).

Site Setup

Maybe you already have a concrete patio and you're tired of looking at its plain surface. Even if the concrete is old and slightly deteriorated, it may still be usable, and a stone patio will protect the concrete from further decay. For the concrete pad to be suitable, it should be intact, with no large open cracks or sections that have actually separated from the larger mass. Small cracks and areas where concrete has chipped away from the surface are acceptable. They'll get filled in with mortar as you set the flagstone.

An old concrete surface will need to be cleaned to ensure that the mortar adheres properly. Scouring the concrete surface with a bleach and water solution and a stiff brush is one way. You can also have the surface pressure-washed. For removing algae buildup, spilled oils, and other contaminants, apply a solution of hydro chloric (muriatic) acid and water mixed in equal parts. Use a stiff fiber brush on a long handle to spread the solution and scrub stubborn areas. Thoroughly rinse the surface with water. When using muriatic acid, follow the directions on the container. Use extreme caution when handling the acid, and wear rubber gloves and eye protection when applying this solution.

Creating Your Own Concrete Pad

Setting mortared flagstone is a doable project for most anyone; setting up for and pouring the concrete pad

Random pieces of blue sandstone flagging are set in an eye-catching design. The mortared flagstone surface is durable and relatively maintenance-free.

may be a stretch for some people. If this is the case, you may want to hire a mason or carpenter to do the concrete work for you. Follow the instructions on pages 99–102 and the information on creating a form for pouring the pad yourself.

Staking out the Pad's Perimeter

See page 73. But in this case, make sure to mark the perimeter outside your planned area, since you're pouring a concrete pad, which requires the use of plywood forms. See pages 75–76 for information on determining the pitch, and grading the site. If you have a concrete pad in place and it's not pitched, you can create a pitch to the stone surface by starting with a thicker base of mortar at one end and decreasing the amount beneath the stones as you move to the opposite end.

Building the Form

Once you have graded the site and created the proper pitch, you need to create the form work to hold in the concrete. The upper edge of the form work represents where the top of the concrete pad will be. It's critical to get this edge set correctly to accommodate the thickness of the pad. The form work doesn't have to be beautiful, but it does need to be strong enough to contain the concrete during pouring without bowing or moving. Dimensions for your pad's form work will be specific to your site, as the forms are built into the area you created for the pad.

Begin by using a circular saw to rip 4-inch-tall (10.2-cm) pieces of ⅜-inch (1-cm) plywood that match the dimensions of your graded area. You'll need only three lengths if your fourth wall is the home's foundation. For this side, you'll need pressure-treated expansion joint material, which you'll place between the poured concrete and the wall. If your design involves curves, hose the plywood down a couple of times; it bends easily when wet. Then pound 12-inch (30.5-cm) 2×4 or 2×2

Four-inch-wide (10.2-cm) strips of plywood supported by narrow stakes mark the perimeter for the concrete pad that will be poured for a flagstone patio.

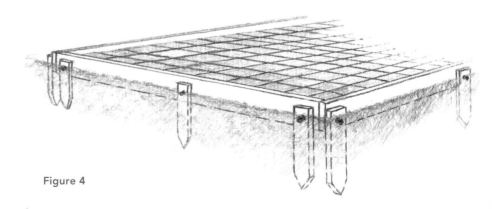

Figure 4

stakes into the ground. Place the stakes along the outside of the plywood every 2 feet (0.6 m), with extra at the corners. Drive screws to secure the forms to the stakes (figure 4).

Steel-toothed landscaping rakes can be used to evenly distribute poured concrete.

Pieces of flagstone being dry-fit before they're set in mortar.

Pouring the Concrete

See page 100–102 for detailed instructions on pouring concrete. You'll suspend heavy-gauge reinforcing wire in the middle of the concrete pad. If the pad receives minor cracks, the wire is there to hold the concrete in place.

Once your concrete pad is in place, allow it to cure for 48 hours before working on top of it. If the weather is hot and dry, keep the pad damp so the concrete will cure slowly. Spray the concrete surface several times during the day for two days from the point it has set up enough so that the water won't wash away the surface of the concrete.

Removing the Form Work

After the concrete has set up for 24 hours, you can remove the form work. Unscrew the stakes and pry the strips away from the concrete.

Dry-Fitting the Flagging

Dry-fitting a section of paving gives you time to get the desired fit between the flagstones before you set them in mortar. At the top of the pitched site, start at a corner or along an outside edge of the pad and work your way across the pad. You want to start along the top edge of the sloped pad so that if it rains you can cover your work and not worry about the rainwater running down the slope into fresh mortar. The same holds true if you need to hose down the pad or stones while working.

Begin with a 4-foot-square (0.36 m²) area. Look for angles and curves that complement each other and line them up together. Once you have a few pieces laid out, it's easier to see how other pieces will work in the puzzle. Pieces with long straight edges work well along the outside edges of the concrete pad. Blend the larger pieces with the medium and smaller ones. Look for pieces that have at least one matching edge to the pieces already laid out. If a portion of one piece overlaps another one you've already laid out, you'll need to mark and break away that portion. Don't forget to leave room for mortar joints. If you're laying a totally random pattern, you won't need to be as critical with the placement of the flagging or the width of the mortar joints.

Setting the Flagging in Mortar

To mortar the pieces in place, you'll have to move them from the dry-fit position in order to spread the mortar (take a mental picture of the layout before moving the pieces). When you're first starting out, you may want to use a crayon or piece of chalk to mark along the outside edge of the pieces you have dry-fit. This will give you a reference point for spreading the mortar. Work with four to six pieces at a time. See page 104 for instructions on mixing mortar.

Using a shovel, place a couple scoops of mortar onto the pad where you have just removed the dry-fit flagstone. Spread the mortar out with a trowel to a minimum thickness of 1 inch (2.5 cm). Thinner flaggings will need more mortar, while the thicker pieces will require less.

Select an outside edge or corner piece from the dry-fit section and lay it down on top of the bed of mortar, pressing it into the mortar, and you're on your way. If the mortar is the correct consistency, you'll be able to push the stone into the mortar. If it's a bit stiff, you may need a rubber mallet to encourage it into place.

Checking for Pitch and Level

Use the 4-foot (1.2-m) level to check the pitch of the piece's surface with the necessary slope, then turn the level 90-degree to check for level. Depending on how even the surface of a piece is, you may have to move the level around, taking several readings for a particular area and working with an average reading. After setting a

Use stones with long, straight edges to work along the perimeter of square and rectangular concrete pads.

few sections of dry-fit stones, you'll be able to set the pieces by eye and then double check by using the level. With the first section of flagging set in mortar, you'll be ready to go on and dry-fit another section.

Other Considerations

■ As you work the flagging into place, you'll notice that along the outside edge of the section you're setting there will be small amounts of extra mortar left from when you pushed a piece of flagstone into place. Keep this mortar cut back flush with the outside edges of the pieces you have just laid. Use your trowel to cut the mortar back to be reused. Make sure the mortar is cut back along this edge at the end of a working session so you have a clean edge to work up to when you return.

- If you're working in shade or partial shade, the mortar, the pad's surface, and the stones will be cooler, allowing for plenty of working time. If a batch of mortar is wetter than necessary, let it set for five to ten minutes before setting the flagging. You can then work on dry-fitting another section. When working in direct sun on a hot, dry day, the mortar sets up much more quickly. One way to slow things down is to occasionally use a hose to mist the stones and the pad. A damp concrete pad and damp stones are fine; though you don't want the concrete pad soaking wet with standing water when you're ready to spread mortar.

- Once a batch of mortar is mixed, it needs to be used within about one hour, depending on how wet the mortar is. To keep the mortar from drying out too quickly, keep it consolidated in a mass in the wheelbarrow or mortar pan and cover it with a folded tarp or scrap of plywood.

Grouting the Mortar Joints

There are a couple of ways to grout your mortar joints. One is to do the grouting as you go along, which makes a better bonding of mortar between the joints and the concrete pad. On larger projects, this is best accomplished by having one person set the flagging and another grout the joints. If you're working alone, grouting slows the process of getting the pieces set in place, as it can get a bit tedious. You can save grouting until the end of the project and get the satisfaction of laying the stones out first. If you do this, be sure to leave the joints fairly clean of mortar, while leaving the mortar at the bottom of each joint alone.

Use a level to check the angle of each stone as it's set.

Once a piece is set, cut away the excess mortar around its edges. Be sure that the mortar is flush with the edges of the stone at the end of each working session so you'll have a clean edge when you resume work on the project.

Though it's not hard or heavy work, grouting does take some concentration while you're in a sitting or kneeling position. Kneepads or garden pads made of dense foam are a must when grouting.

Grouting Techniques

Work the mortar between the joints with a pointing trowel or a small duckbill trowel. A small section of plywood, a short section of scrap 2 × 10 lumber, or one of the pavers works well to spread on the mortar for grouting. Place approximately 1 quart (0.95 l) of mortar on your board and spread it out evenly about 1 inch (2.5 cm) thick in a more or less rectangular shape.

With your trowel, cut away a narrow strip of mortar about the width of the mortar joint you're working on. The mortar should be stiff enough to hold this shape. Work the mortar into the joint, pushing it down along the length of the joint. Add more until the mortar is even with the surface of the stones. Take your time and keep the amount of smeared mortar on the surface of the stones to a minimum. Immediately wipe away any mortar that does smear with a sponge or wet rag. Work the mortar with your trowel until the surface of the mortar is even and fairly smooth.

When you're setting the first couple sections of flagstone, the mortar joints will be filled while working on top of the concrete pad. The mortared flagging will need to set up for one hour on a warm and dry day, and more if it is a cold and damp day, before you can put your weight on them. Carefully step or kneel on the center of the larger flagstones to avoid putting pressure on their edges and the smaller pieces until they have cured for half a day.

Brushed and Smooth Mortar Joints

There are a couple of ways to treat the surface of the grouted mortar. One is to leave it smooth after you trowel the joint. A smooth mortar joint tends to show the trowel marks easily, and you may actually like that look. Another option is to lightly brush the grout surface with a flexible bristle brush. To do this, allow the smooth mortar to set up until it loses its glossy

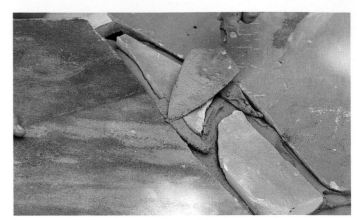

Use a pointing trowel to cut away sections of mortar about the thickness of the joint you're filling. Work the mortar into the joint. It should be flush with the surfaces of the flagstones.

Press down firmly with the trowel to completely fill the joint with mortar.

Finish the joint's upper surface by leaving it troweled and smooth, or wait for the mortar to lose its watery sheen and then brush its surface with a masonry brush for a grainy finish.

A fire ring accents this mortared flagstone patio.

sheen. Then lightly brush over the mortar until it has a coarse look to it. A coarse finish hides trowel marks left in the joint and looks a little more subdued than the smooth sheen. Both finishes are fine; it really depends on your preference. Try a little of each at the beginning of the project, and then, for the sake of a consistent look, stick with one.

Final Thoughts

- Keep your work area swept clean, particularly areas of the pad where you're about to spread mortar and set flagstones.

- Cover newly finished paving if the weather is extremely hot, dry, and windy, or if it's about to rain. Covering the work will slow the setting-up time and the mortar's curing process, which reduces cracks in the mortar and improves the bonding of mortar and stone.

- Allow the mortar to cure for several days before you put any furniture on a newly paved surface.

Creating a Fire Ring

Fire rings are used to keep a fire contained in a designated area. A successful fire ring on a patio needs a hole in the concrete pad that allows rainwater to filter through. Without the hole, rainwater would fill the ring and cause ashes and charred wood to float out and across the patio.

Decide where you want your ring and create the necessary form work around the area you planned for the ring. When you're designing a fire ring, special consideration needs to be given to the size of the fires you'd like to have. The interior diameter of the fire ring pictured here is roughly 30 inches (76.2 cm). Any ring smaller than 24 inches (61 cm) in diameter will permit only relatively small wood to be used.

Pour the concrete for the pad, and remove the form work used to create the ring 48 hours later. Dig an 18-inch (45.7-cm) hole in the circle using a posthole digger and a shovel. Fill the hole with 8 to 10 inches (20.3 to 25.4 cm) (depending on how deep you want your "pit" to be) of 1-inch (2.5-cm) gravel.

Dry lay the stones first.

Use a pointed trowel to work the mortar around the stones.

Set the tallest stone first and use different amounts of mortar to fit the rest of the stones to the same height as the first stone.

Use metamorphic or igneous stone for your ring, and make sure the rocks are similar in height and shape with edges that match up well. Avoid extremely soft stones that will crumble when exposed to extreme heat. Keep the height of the stones between 8 to 10 inches (20.3 to 25.4 cm), making it easier to work on the fire while allowing more light to spill out from the ring.

Dry-fit the stones first. Place them on the edge of the concrete pad and use wedges to keep the stones from falling over. Once you're satisfied with the look of the ring, mix your mortar (use the recipe on page 103) and begin mortaring your ring in place. Remove your tallest stone first and place a 2-inch (5.1-cm) base of mortar on the exposed section of pad. Push the stone into the mortar and carefully pack the mortar around the base of the stone on the inside and outside of the ring. Work the mortar around the base of the stone up to 2 inches (5.1 cm). Set the remaining stones using a level to adjust their height and extra mortar to make them level to the tallest stone. After the stones are mortared into place, set the flagstone for the patio right up to the outside of the ring (masking the exposed mortar).

Paving an Interior Hearth

The hearth pictured on the facing page is one that I built for my friends Jackie and Evan in their new home. Evan built the house and worked with me on this project. The hearth took us about half a day to complete. Its design can be adapted to fit most any situation involving a freestanding wood stove or a vented gas-burning unit. The stone for the hearth is a locally quarried, metamorphosed granite and shist rock with obvious bands of quartz and speckled mica throughout its structure. The wood-burning stove sitting on the completed hearth has a soapstone exterior.

This simple stone hearth can be altered to fit almost any interior setting.

Cement Board

Interior cement board is a rigid material made of a aggregated portland cement core with a fiberglass mesh coating. It's typically used in house construction as a masonry surface for applying ceramic tile. It comes in 3 × 4 or 3 × 5-foot (0.9 × 1.2 or 0.9 × 1.5-m) sheets with a ⁵⁄₁₆- or ½-inch (8-mm or 1.3-cm) thickness and is available at most building supply and home improvement stores.

The cement board is set on top of a ¾-inch (1.9-cm) plywood subfloor, nailed to a doubled-up 2 × 8 floor joist. Evan doubled up the floor joist directly beneath the hearth area to handle the extra weight of the stone and a 400-pound (182 kg) stove. If you're setting a hearth on a wood-framed floor, consult with a carpenter or building contractor for a professional opinion of how to deal with the extra weight in your particular situation.

Setting the Cement Board

Mark the measurements of your hearth's design on the subfloor using a tape measure and a chalk box to strike the lines, or a pencil and a 4-foot (1.2-m) level as a straight edge to make your marks, then cut the cement board to fit in this area. You can score the cement board with a utility knife and break it along the scored line. Or use a jigsaw with a masonry blade, which allows you to cut with more control.

To provide an absolutely even surface for the cement board, spread a ½-inch (1.3-cm) layer of latex-fortified mortar (follow the directions provided on the bag), using a notched tile-setter's trowel. Lay the cement board down and secure it in place with 1½-inch (3.8-cm) roofing tacks or all-purpose screws.

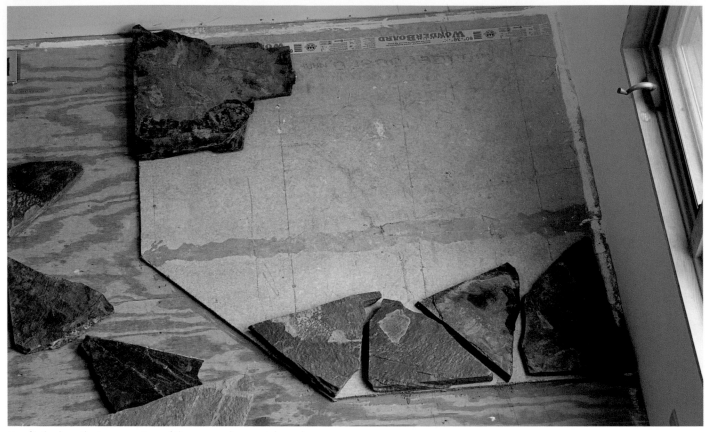

Dry fit the hearth stones on top of the secured cement board.

Stone Selection

Stones with an even surface provide a more stable area on which to set the wood stove and will be easier to keep clean. Stones with major protrusions and uneven surfaces may require some shimming under the stove's legs to secure them. The stone used for the hearth pictured here averaged 1½ inches (3.8 cm) in thickness. Fieldstone, flagstone, and slate will all work for this project.

Dry-Fitting the Stones

Start dry-fitting the stones around the perimeter of the cement board, then work toward the center. Trim the stone's edges, when necessary, to create joints that average ¾ inch (1.9 cm). Check for level before continuing.

Mortaring the Stones

To set the stones, mix a batch of mortar described on page 103, and follow the directions for setting flagstone

Dry fit smaller pieces of stone in the gaps.

on pages 123–126. The mortared joints in this project were completed with a brushed finish (pages 126–127) To complete the project, Evan used a band of red oak trim to frame the hearth and match the oak flooring.

Special Consideration

If the wood stove is extremely close to a wall, a fire barrier is required to satisfy fire safety codes. Check with your building inspector for local requirements.

A red oak trim was added after the stones were mortared but before the joints were grouted.

CHAPTER SIX

PLANTS AND STONE

Plants and stones are natural partners. When they're combined properly, they continue to complement each other season after season. A grouping of stones, whether arranged by Mother Nature herself or by hand, can provide a perfect niche or backdrop for green and colorful growth. Sometimes plants and stones look so congenial together, it's hard to decide which showed up first.

In some naturalized settings, delicate plants such as these Mexican evening primroses appear to be growing straight from the rocks.

Perennials spill over the tapered end of a dry-stacked boulder wall.

Selecting Plants

To find out which plants will do best in your region and in rocky environments, visit your local garden center and study a few books and plant catalogues. Of course, the specific location of your stone project will have some bearing on the plants you choose. Ask yourself whether the plants will sit in full sunlight, dense shade, or partial shade. Is the soil well drained or is it usually damp? Is it acid or alkaline? Will the project be exposed to harsh winds or located in a well-protected area? Stonecrops and many alpine plants do fine on windy hillsides, whereas tender woodland plants prefer dappled sunlight and a more tranquil setting.

Consider using plants that are native to your area. These will help your wall blend in with the surrounding environment. Be careful to choose varieties that will thrive in the conditions provided by your stonescaping site.

Many nurseries offer native plants. You may also gather them from the wild, but if you do, take only varieties that grow in abundance and leave plenty of healthy plants behind. Also remember to get permission from the landowner if you're gathering on property that is not your own.

You'll find more tips on plant selection in the following sections.

These grey stone surfaces contrast pleasantly with the lush green and vibrant blooms of an Olympic Fire mountain laurel.

Plants and Dry-Stacked Stone Walls

The soil in front of and above your retaining wall, whether it's level or sloped, often makes a fine setting for a garden bed. Plants may also be set directly into the wall.

When set along the base of the wall, plants serve as a visual anchor for the stone structure. If planted above the wall or within the upper stone courses, cascading varieties such as trailing cranberries, dianthus, and alpine strawberries will hide some stones while highlighting others.

Some gardeners enjoy the lush and informal look of heavy growth. They select varieties that will drape down luxuriously over the stones and fill the beds above

them with eye-catching color. Other gardeners prefer a sparser and more formal look, one that emphasizes the stones rather than the plant growth.

The best time to set plants right into the joints of your stone wall or paving project is while you're stacking or laying the stones. This won't work, of course, if you're working when the temperatures are too cold for tender young plants.

To set plants directly within a wall, leave a gap between two stones as you're laying a course. This gap must be wide enough to hold the plant's crown (the portion of the plant between its roots and leaves) and a little soil.

Many plants, such as these alpine strawberries, do well in retaining walls.

When setting a plant in a wall, recess its crown in a gap between two stones and carefully fan out the roots.

The plant should rest on a trail of soil that extends from the interior of the wall back to the soil bank. To prevent this soil from migrating down through the gravel backfill or out through the face of the wall, you may want to start by spreading some landscape fabric over the gravel and over the gap in the wall stones. Cut a hole in the fabric, locating it at the gap; the roots of the plant that you place in the gap will extend through this hole.

Next, make up a mixture of topsoil, composted manure, coarse sand, and water-absorbing granules. (The granules, available at nurseries and garden stores, absorb available moisture and release it gradually into the soil.) You'll need about 3 gallons (11.4 l) of this soil mixture for each plant you set. Spread about 2 gallons (7.6 l) over

the fabric, from the back of the wall to the soil bank. This trail of planting medium will nurture the plant as its roots reach back for the nutrients and moisture in the soil bank.

Place the plant in the gap, with its crown about 2 inches (5 cm) in from the face of the wall. (Recessing the crown in this manner will protect it from harsh, drying winds.) Insert the plant's crown through the hole in the landscape fabric and carefully fan out the roots on top of the trail of soil. Place another gallon (3.8 l) of the soil mixture on top of the roots and water the entire area well. Then continue setting more wall stones. The gravel backfill that you add behind subsequent courses will bury the soil surrounding the roots of the plants.

Two large chunks of schist rock make a comfortable spot for sitting beneath a northern grey birch, which shades a variety of woodland perennials and colorful annuals.

Boulders and stacked stones are the dominant features in this arid southwestern garden.

Located in a moist, temperate region, the stones in this winding wall are almost obscured by lush summer growth.

Following are a few tips on planting in and around stone walls:

- If your wall sits in full sun, protect the transplants for several days by placing a couple of boards up against the wall at an angle. Draping a piece of burlap down from the top of the wall will also work.

- Plants set just in front of your wall may receive the extra moisture that drains down through the gravel backfill. Be careful not to overwater them.

- Unless your wall has a full southern exposure, a planting bed at its base is likely to be shady. If your wall does face south, the stones in it will retain heat, so soil temperatures close to the wall will be quite warm.

- If any part of your wall will also serve as a bench, avoid setting plants in areas where dangling legs might damage them.

- Unless you want to see more plants than stones, avoid over-planting. Although young seedlings will look quite sparse during their first season, their foliage will grow significantly during the second and third.

- Small groups of plants, placed in the wall randomly, look more natural than evenly spaced arrangements.

- Plant varieties that require well-drained soil (alpines and stonecrops are two good examples) do especially well in dry-stacked walls because the gravel backfill guarantees good drainage.

- Woodland plants are happiest in a rich, moist soil. To help retain moisture in their planting medium, be sure to add water-absorbing granules to it.

- Water the plants regularly, especially during their first growing season. The immature roots of young seedlings can't reach back into the soil bank behind the wall, so they'll need your help until they can.

Creeping plants such as Irish moss quickly cover the gaps between stones.

Plants and Stone Paving

Plants set into the joints of a paved area or around its edges have both practical and aesthetic advantages. By blending stone pavers in with surrounding vegetation, greenery helps soften the visual impact of hard stone surfaces. In addition, plants set within the joints of a patio, walkway, or courtyard help discourage the growth of weeds in these areas by crowding them out. If you select hardy aromatic varieties, you'll also enjoy the marvelous scents they release when they're crushed.

Among the best plants for areas such as paving or steps are creeping varieties that will withstand heavy foot traffic. The leaves of some—including chamomile, fragrant thymes, winter savory, Corsican mint, and low-growing alpines—will also release fragrant

For beds above low retaining walls, choose low-growing plants rather than draping plants that might hide the stones completely.

Within two or three years, the young woolly thyme seedlings planted in the gaps among these fieldstone pavers will spread profusely.

aromas when they're crushed by passing feet. These plants will spread throughout the joints in paved areas and will be kept "pruned" by the people and pets who tread on them.

Usually, pavers are set on gravel beds, and the gaps between them are filled with gravel. As you lay out the pavers, choose a few gaps for planting and instead of filling them, remove the gravel bed from the bottom of each one. Next, mix up some soil, compost, and coarse sand. Then sprinkle some water-absorbing granules in the bottom of the gap. Add some of the soil mixture on top of the granules, set the plant, and add more soil mixture as necessary to fill the gap. (Make sure you place the granules below the soil mixture. I once made the mistake of sprinkling them in the upper layer of soil, and the first heavy rain scattered little granule islands all over the stone patio!)

Water the young seedlings frequently, as the gravel bed beneath the paving will drain moisture away quickly.

Planters and Tree Wells

Planters and tree wells are simply dry-stacked retaining walls that serve specific functions. The crescent-shaped planters shown on this page were set into existing slopes and filled with layers of lightly tamped soil as the courses of stone were stacked. (Tamping the soil prevents dramatic settling later.) On a level lawn, the walls of a dry-stacked planter should encircle the planting bed completely.

A tree well is a great solution to a problem that often arises during excavation of a building, driveway, or road site. When excavated soil is carelessly mounded around the base of a tree, the tree gradually suffocates. Removing this soil from around the trunk and dry-stacking a tree well to retain the soil at a safe distance can save a tree's life. (Leave plenty of room around the trunk for future growth.)

The thriving sedum set in this flight of steps helps soften the hard-edged appearance of the stones.

Plants and Stone Steps

Plants may be set along the edges of stone steps, between the risers and treads, and within any gaps between stones. Avoid placing large, bushy varieties along the sides of steps, or you'll end up spending more time clearing away the overgrowth than you do setting the stones! For gaps between risers and treads, select hardier varieties, such as fragrant miniature alpine plants and hardy, aromatic "creepers." Tender varieties won't survive foot traffic; they'll do better along the edges.

Hosta and delicate maidenhair ferns complement the rounded river
rocks and carpet of moss in the foreground.

Revealing a Stone Ledge

I once spent a day uncovering a large, partly exposed rock ledge for a client. First, I removed some vines
and raked away plant debris. Then, with a digging spade and mattock, I removed the topsoil, which I set
aside for later use. I also removed all the loose stones around the face of the ledge.

As the work progressed, I used smaller tools. The tapered blade of a brick mason's hammer, a mason's
trowel, and a broom helped remove the soil from tight crevices. At this stage, I felt like an archaeologist,
unearthing the skeleton of a huge prehistoric creature. By the time I'd finished, what I'd thought was one
very large stone turned out to be a series of three linked rock faces that spanned 20 feet (6 m).

After I cleared the stone faces, I combined the saved topsoil with compost and used the mixture to
make a bed for bulbs in front of the ledge. Every spring, the ledge serves as a beautiful backdrop for a
variety of daffodils and tulips.

Naturalizing with Stone

Single stones or groupings of stones can transform an otherwise ordinary plot into a breathtakingly beautiful landscape. If you're lucky, your property will have large boulders, ledges, or natural stone outcroppings on it already. Often, these are buried, but transforming them into stunning landscape highlights is a simple matter of removing soil from around them and then adding plants.

If your land isn't rich with stone already, a stone yard can provide the rocks you need. Moving and setting boulders requires heavy equipment, of course, so before you spend any money having large stones delivered and arranged, make sure that your own property isn't hiding any. Take a walk around your land, keeping an eye peeled for the occasional rock jutting out of a sloping area or the barely exposed surfaces of rocks buried beneath the soil. With a bit of digging, buried boulders, stone outcroppings, and rock ledges can be brought to daylight.

Once you've revealed part of a buried rock, arranging large or small stones of a similar kind around it can complement this portion of your landscape. You're quite likely to find these additional stones nearby, but if you don't, search at the stone yard for closely matching stones.

It's also possible to assemble a natural-looking outcropping for alpines or other low-growing plants with boulders and stones. A gentle slope is the best site for projects of this kind. If you don't have an existing slope on your property, just make one by building up the soil.

Keep these stone arrangements simple and position the stones far enough apart to leave room for plants among them. Use native stones when you can, positioning large slabs with their back surfaces buried in

A creative arrangement of colorful plants and huge boulders makes a stunning, naturalized landscape.

This small boulder garden was created by importing and arranging rocks from a stone yard.

Given time, plants set among rocks will reduce competition from sprouting weed seeds. Coreopsis and rhododendron complement these large boulders.

soil or scree (loose rock debris) as if the slabs were part of a naturally developed stratum.

Backfill the areas behind the stones with a mixture of soil and gravel or scree. Adjust the mixture to meet the acidity requirements of the plants you intend to set in it. Your local agricultural extension agent can provide you with information on how to test your soil and make the necessary adjustments.

To prepare small planting beds in any grouping of rocks, create pockets of topsoil and compost (or soil and scree) on the uphill sides of the stones. These miniature gardens, planted with ground covers or alpines, will enhance the exposed rock surfaces. Add a few dwarf conifers and a simple stone bench to complete the picture. To link an area like this with another part of your landscape, build a stepping-stone path between the two.

The photos on the next page show two portions of a naturalized garden project that was years in the making and that is still evolving. Located at an elevation of 4,000 feet (1219 m), this garden serves as a privacy screen for a house tucked between two other houses on a narrow lot.

The design required the creation of several carefully placed hillocks. These were made by combining packed clay soil and large boulders, and included pockets of amended soil to hold a variety of plants. The hillock shown in the upper photo on this page rises dramatically to 10 feet (3 m) in height.

In the lower photo, weathered stones and evergreens offer year-round beauty while gracefully retaining a low bank of soil. Because many stones in this project were very large and heavy, they had to be set with the help of a tractor. To create a similar project on a smaller scale—one that won't require the use of heavy equipment—just use smaller stones.

Several people created this naturalized garden project, which is located in the mountains of western North Carolina. The moss-covered stones, ferns, and rhododendron all mimic a natural woodland environment.

This border was created with weathered pieces of sandstone.

Round, irregular stones border this garden's perimeter. The ones in the center double as stepping stones.

Borders

For a very deliberate and attractive looking border to surround a garden bed, look for stones with two flat sides that are of a similar thickness when stood on their narrower edge. These stones should be twice the height of the finished border. For example, if you want 5 inches (12.7 cm) of stone revealed above ground, the stone should have 5 inches (12.7 cm) below ground for a height totaling 10 inches (25.4 cm).

Start at one end of the garden bed or path and dig a short length of trench wide enough to set the stones into. A shovel or posthole digger works well for this type of digging. Set the topsoil off to one side. The subsoil can be shoveled into a wheelbarrow and set out of the way.

Lay out six to eight stones, matching the ends that fit together well. Stand them up on edge in the trench and adjust their heights as needed using a level as a guide. Pour gravel or soil under the shorter ones. When the stones are set the way you want, fill in around their sides with the gravel or the topsoil, and pack the soil down with a tamper.

Small, rough boulders create a raised bed for perennials and a Japanese maple at Warren Wilson College, Swannanoa, North Carolina.

Circular planting beds were created with a mix of large and small rubble stones. The larger stones are set in a shallow trench; smaller stones are used to even out the height of the border.

CHAPTER SEVEN

STONES AND WATER

For thousands of years, people have devised ways to contain, transport, and use water. This wonderful substance is necessary, of course, but it's also naturally beautiful. The projects in this chapter make it possible to enjoy the alluring sight and sound of water on your property.

A Stone Niche for a Spigot

This spigot-and-stonework project is set along a wood-land path at Winterberry Farm in Haywood County, North Carolina. Its location makes watering woodland seedlings on the farm easy. The stonework serves two functions—one practical and one aesthetic. The stone shelf below the spigot holds a bucket or watering can, and the niche provides an attractive landmark as well.

The stones I had on hand (culls from another project) and the nature of the site itself (secluded, heavily shaded, and rich with plant life) determined the informal, rustic style of the stonework. In a different setting and with different stones, I might have chosen to dry-stack the stones to create a retaining wall within the cut bank, using the shelf as its base.

Preparing the Site

First, you must run a plastic plumbing pipe from a water source to your project site. (If you're not comfortable doing this job yourself, you'll need to hire a plumber.) The trench for the pipe should be 1 to 3 feet (30 to 91 cm) deep, depending on the depth to which the ground freezes.

During the cold months of the year, the water is turned off and the line drained. It's possible to create an all-season spigot by insulating the pipe or using what's known as a "stand-up" pipe instead.

Figure 2

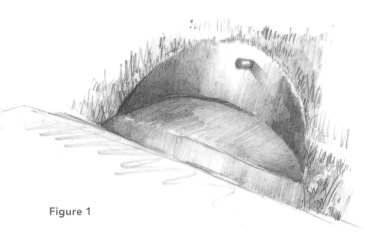

Figure 1

Use large stones to build up the sides of the structure. Then, working from one side of the niche to the other, shape a simple arch by stepping the stones over the vertical stone. Use the edges of these stones to lock the vertical stone in place. Slip the spigot into the end of the pipe and attach it with a stainless-steel clamp (figure 3).

Next, dig a 4-foot-long (1.2-m) and 2 ½-foot-wide (76-cm) shelf into the bank. To make reaching the spigot easy, the shelf should rest about 1 foot (30 cm) above path level (figure 1).

Laying the Stone

Spread a 2-inch-thick (5 cm) bed of gravel over the excavated shelf. Next, set one or two large, flat stones on the gravel. These should cover the shelf and overlap it by about 4 inches (10 cm). Then, position a very large, heavy stone on the back ends of the two shelf stones, tilting it slightly back toward the bank. Position the end of the pipe on top of this stone, leaving several inches hanging over the edge (figure 2).

Figure 3

Building a Dry-Laid Stone Culvert

A culvert is a drainpipe beneath a road or driveway; it diverts water from one location to another. Culverts catch and redirect water from roadside drainage ditches and prevent flooded roads during heavy storms.

The project shown on the opposite page is a stone retaining structure for the intake end of a culvert pipe that directs water from a ditch along one side of a road to a ditch on the other side. The stones prevent the banks of the ditch from eroding and also improve the area's appearance.

Selecting Stones

Large flat stones set on edge will do the best job of directing water from the ditch into the pipe. Alternatively, you may stack stones as you would when building a wall, but be sure to use large block-shaped stones along the bottom course. Smaller stones may be dislodged by the force of moving water.

Preparing the Site

First cut back the sides of the ditch. Make these cuts deep enough to accommodate the stones you'll be using and angle them back about 5 to 10 degrees, so the stones you set against the bank will be battered. The cut at the end of the ditch should be deep enough to hold a large stone, positioned on edge, between the bank and the culvert pipe (figure 4).

Setting the Stones

Moving water will hit the end wall wth the most force, so use a stone with a large face to cover it. Set this stone on end, leaning it against the bank, with its face contacting the exposed edge of the pipe. Fill any gaps between this stone and the bank with packed soil or gravel. If this first stone doesn't extend to the opposite corner, fill the gap with other stones. Then continue setting stones along the bank, working around the corner and down the sides and backfilling with gravel as you go. To cover the bank around the pipe, set a low, short run of stones, either standing them on edge or

Figure 4

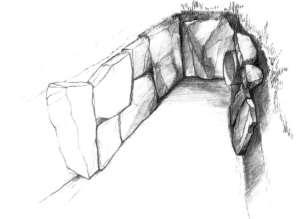

Figure 5

stacking them (figure 5). Finally, set large capstones over the upper edges of the stones already in place (figure 6).

To secure the discharge end of the pipe, just dry-stack a low stone wall around the pipe's opening or stabilize the pipe with large rubble stones.

Annual Maintenance

At least once a year, clean out any accumulated leaves or debris from the base of the stonework surrounding the intake end of the pipe. Lining the bottom of the ditch with rubble will dissipate the force of the rushing water, but I find it much easier to remove debris with a rake and shovel when the soil is bare.

Figure 6

Reworking a Creek Culvert

Many property owners with driveways that cross over creeks or streams already have culvert pipes in place. In this project, you'll learn how to construct dry-stacked walls around the intake end of one of these pipes.

The 4-foot-diameter (1.2-m) culvert shown in the photo above allows a creek to run beneath my driveway. When I first moved to the property, the outflow end of the culvert—a concrete-block wall faced with stone—was still in good shape. The dry-stacked stonework at the inflow end, however, had collapsed into piles of stone on both sides of the pipe's opening, and the slope from the driveway down to the top of the pipe was

caving in. The simplest and most practical solution was to stabilize the bank by dismantling the old stonework and restacking the stone walls.

One tip before you start a similar project: Unless the creek or ditch is dry, there's no way to avoid getting wet as you build the stone walls of a culvert! You'll be standing right in the bed of the creek or ditch as you work. To minimize sogginess, wear a pair of tall rubber boots. Making a few walkways by placing boards just above water level will also help.

Dismantling the Old Stonework

I started work when the creek was low. First, I completely dismantled the old stonework on the right-hand side of the inlet end. In order to redirect some of the creek water away from my work area and off to the left, I removed some of the largest stones and placed them in the creek itself.

Some of the original stones were suitable for restacking. The others, irregular in shape, were good backfill material, so I saved them to thicken the new wall and add to its ballast. To supplement the useable recycled stones, I handpicked about ½ ton (508 kg) of stone at a stone yard.

Stacking Flared Wing Walls

During heavy spring rains, the volume of this creek increases dramatically. Sometimes, the water level reaches the bottom edges of the capstones on the right-hand side of the culvert, in front of the hemlock tree. I therefore decided to build dramatically flared new walls—ones that would funnel this rush of water into the pipe. Because the water flow is sometimes extremely heavy, I also knew I'd have to use very large stones.

I dry-stacked the right-hand wall first. I started by wedging stones between the outside surface of the pipe's opening and the soil bank to make sure that water wouldn't flow behind the pipe. Then, to clear a site for the first course of the wall, I removed a few stones that jutted out from the creek bed. Next, I laid out the first course of the wall by placing some of my largest stones directly into the creek.

As I stacked this wall, I set the first stone in each course to overlap the lip of the pipe. I also rounded the wall dramatically in order to make sure that water flowing out of a smaller creek on the right would hit stones rather than soil as it entered the larger creek. To backfill the wall, I combined the irregularly shaped culls that I'd saved with crushed limestone that I had on hand and small stones gathered from the creek. The creek was also a good source for shims, wedges, and the smaller stones across the top of the pipe.

As I continued to stack courses, I had to remove the lower branches of the hemlock tree in order to provide working space. I took care to leave enough soil and space for the tree's future growth.

After capping off the section of the wall in front of the tree, I cut a shelf in the bank behind the tree and stacked a couple of courses of that wall. Then I shifted my attention to the wall on the left-hand side of the creek.

First, I had to move the water-diverting stones that I'd set in the creek. I placed these at the opposite side to divert water from my new work area at the left-hand side of the culvert. Then I stacked the new wall, using my largest stones in the bottom course and backfilling as before.

The final stage of this project was stacking the wall just beneath the road, which I did in the usual fashion.

Working with New Culvert Pipe

If you have a small creek on your property and would like to install a culvert pipe with a pathway over it, try the following project. If, however, your creek is large and you want to build a driveway over the culvert, I strongly recommend that you consult with a professional. You can certainly dry-stack the stones at the ends of a large culvert, but setting the pipe, gravel, and road bond will require the use of heavy equipment. For smaller projects, you'll only need a pick-up truck to haul the pipe, gravel, and stones.

Culvert pipe is cylindrical in shape and made of rigid plastic or heavy-gauge galvanized steel. Diameters can range from 1 to 10 feet (30 to 305 cm). To create a 6-foot-wide (183 cm) path over a small creek, a pipe 10 feet long and 3 feet (91 cm) or smaller in diameter will be sufficient. To find a local supplier, just look in your telephone book, under "Pipes" or "Culverts."

Have the pipe cut to length before you pick it up or before it's delivered. Most pipe sellers will deliver, but if you don't want to pay for this service, a small truck can usually transport short sections. You can join these with a connector once they're at your site. Elbow sections that allow pipes to be joined at 90- and 45-degree angles are also available.

Determining the diameter of the pipe you'll need is tricky, as there's no way to gauge exactly how much water will flow through the pipe at any given time. One way to estimate the diameter is to observe the volume of water in the creek after a heavy rainfall. Take note of the water's width and depth at the spot where you want to set the culvert; your culvert pipe must be able to cope with that volume of water.

Order a pipe the diameter of which is slightly larger than the diameter you think you need; you never know when the hundred-year flood will hit! If your creek is small and the culvert site is close to its head-waters (where the creek begins), the volume of water may not change drastically from season to season or day to day. If, on the other hand, the site is below a number of tributaries that feed into your creek, or if much new development is taking place upstream, the water can rise dramatically.

Setting the Pipe in Place

Work on this project during a dry season, when the water level in the creek or stream is low. For tips on keeping dry as you work, see page 156.

As you visualize the finished project, keep in mind that the bottom lip of the culvert pipe should sit at or slightly below the bottom of the creek bed. The pipe should slope slightly downward from its intake end to its discharge end.

Start by clearing out any rocks that protrude from the creek bed; set them aside to use in the walls at each end of the pipe. The creek bed must be free of any material that will keep the pipe from sitting evenly along the bottom. Use ¾-inch (2-cm) gravel to fill any holes left by the rocks you remove.

Next, spread a shallow gravel bed down the center of the creek, sloping it downward toward the discharge end and shaping it slightly to match the contour of the bottom of the pipe. The depression in the gravel will ensure good contact between the bed and pipe. Ideally, the lower lip of the pipe should rest at or slightly below the bottom of the creek at the intake end, so don't make the bed too deep.

To position the pipe on the gravel bed, simply roll it into the creek and adjust it by hand. If you're working with two sections of pipe, band them together with a metal collar after placing them on the gravel bed. (Large diameter pipes must be set by heavy equipment.)

After the pipe is in place, stabilize it by placing a few stones along both sides, 1 foot (30 cm) in from each end. Then, toward the center of the pipe, start pouring and tamping layers of gravel in the spaces between the creek banks and the pipe. Your goal is to create a tightly

A dry-stacked wall made with large stones secures this 9-foot-diameter (2.7-m) culvert at its discharge end.

When the Creek Floods

Some friends of mine live in a beautiful valley with a large creek flowing through it. Shortly after moving in, they noticed that during heavy rains, the 4-foot-diameter (1.2-m) culvert beneath their driveway couldn't handle the volume of water in this creek. Excess water flooded the driveway and eroded its edges.

When the culvert was built, it was more than adequate in size, but substantial development upstream had significantly increased the water volume. New rooftops, paved driveways, and other hard surfaces had almost doubled the runoff into the creek. To remedy this situation, my friends widened the creek at their bridge and installed a second, 4-foot-diameter culvert next to the first.

tamped bed that buries most of the pipe and fills the area above it from one side of the creek to the other. Leave enough space at the ends of the pipe to dry-stack walls around the pipe's openings.

Building the Wing and Head Walls

At the inlet end, you'll build angled wing walls that flare out so they'll funnel water into the pipe. The wall at the discharge end will be perpendicular to the pipe rather than flaring outward. Use the instructions in "Reworking A Creek Culvert" (see pages 156–157)

to dry-stack the inlet-end walls first; then stack the wall at the outlet end. As you stack the stones, you'll probably have to add extra gravel behind them to fill the space between their backs and the gravel you poured earlier.

Stack both walls until they're tall enough to ensure that your pathway will be at the height you desire. To stabilize them, add capstones. To make a pathway over the gravel above the culvert, just add a layer of soil, pea gravel, small crushed stone, bark mulch, wood chips, or tamped road bond.

Waterfall Pools

Water—falling, trickling, or streaming across stone surfaces and into pools—creates an atmosphere of tranquility and a refuge from the hectic aspects of our lives. Mirror-like pools speak of passing clouds, catch the golden light of late afternoon, and reflect the many moods of each day. Water gardens are filled with enchantment and change in fascinating ways with every season.

Methods for constructing waterfalls and water gardens vary widely. I've chosen to present only one, but if you're interested in others, you'll find many books on the topic at your local bookstore. Landscape designer and gardener Art Garst created all the landscapes shown in this section, with the exception of the waterfall shown on pages 166 and 167. The project described in the following pages—two pools with water descending from one to the other—is shown on this page. In the sections that follow, you'll find descriptions of the steps Art took as he built this waterfall, but remember as you read them that every site and design will differ. You'll need to study your site carefully and experiment as you set the stones.

Selecting and Preparing the Site

A waterfall project requires a site that is sloped, preferably in a setting that's as natural as possible. As you search for a suitable area, consider the following tips:

- To lengthen a short existing slope, you may be able to build up the area with soil you remove when you excavate a hole for the lower pool.
- To minimize leaf debris, avoid sites beneath or adjacent to large deciduous trees and shrubs.
- Low-lying areas and sites where the water table is close to the surface are invitations to potential flooding.

Falling water splashes over a stone's mossy beard.

plants set within the pools. Annual cleaning (see the section entitled "Pool Maintenance" on page 173) also helps. You may add a commercial biological filter to your pool, available from many garden centers, but this isn't essential.

Gathering the Materials

To build a waterfall similar to the one in this project, you'll need some specific materials.

- The pools shown in the photo on page 164 are lined with EDPM butyl rubber liners. These are usually sold in 10-, 20-, and 30-foot (3-, 6-, and 9-m) widths at nurseries and home-improvement centers, but can be obtained in almost any size.

- To hide and protect the liners below water level, you'll use river rocks, as their rounded edges won't puncture the liner. To cover the portion of each liner that rests above water level, fieldstones or rough-quarried stones with two opposing flat surfaces are best, as you must stack them together tightly.

- A submersible pump moves water from the lower pool to the upper one. Pump sizes vary, depending on how many gallons of water per hour they can handle. The difference in height between your pools will also affect the size you buy. Consult with a pump dealer before making this purchase. The pump that Art used is rated at 1,200 gallons (4,542 l) per hour, at a rise of about 5 feet (1.5 m).

- A length of flexible pipe or garden hose runs from the pump in the lower pool to the upper pool.

Design Considerations

The size and depth of your pools will depend on several factors. One, of course, is the slope of the site itself. Another is whether you want to make a comfortable home for fish. The water in the pools must never freeze solid when the weather turns cold, or your fish won't

- Placing your pools close to your home, where you can see and hear them, will add to your enjoyment. The pools will also be within easy reach when you need to adjust water levels, check on surrounding plants, or feed the fish.

- Selecting an upper pool site that is nearly hidden or disguising the site with plants can give the attractive illusion that your waterfall is fed by a creek.

- Creating a pool environment that will discourage excessive algae growth is very important when you're working with water. Algae growth is inhibited by naturally oxygenated falling water and by

The swirling, recirculated water in the upper pool flows through a channel beneath stacked stones before falling into the larger pool below.

The stone walls lining your pool will be anywhere from 8 to 12 inches (20 to 30 cm) thick. Be sure that the hole you excavate for the pool is large enough, or you'll be disappointed by the pool's finished size.

One warning here: If you don't know whether electrical, plumbing, sewer, or gas lines are buried at your site, check with the utility companies before excavating any soil. Sometimes, these hidden obstacles are easy to move. Your utility company can advise you on this matter.

Preparing the Site

Lay out the circumference of the lower pool first, using garden hoses or sprinkled corn meal. Then remove the vegetation and topsoil from the area inside this line. Also remove vegetation and topsoil from a 1½-foot-wide (46-cm) band outside the marked line. You'll probably disturb the hose line or cornmeal as you do this, so store a mental image of the outline before you start and redefine it when you're finished.

Excavate the topsoil-free area inside the marked line to form a hole that is bowl-shaped at the bottom, with walls that steepen as they rise. As you work, you'll place the soil you remove on top of the 1½-foot-wide band to build up a mounded rim around the site. Pick out and discard any sharp-edged stones and large roots from this soil. You don't want sharp objects in it to puncture the liner.

The rim you build at the lower end of the pool should rise about 1 foot (30 cm) above the desired water level. You may need to use quite a bit of the excavated soil to build up the sloped bank that extends up to the site of the pool above. Obviously, because you're working on a slope, the rim will also slope upward toward the back of the pool.

survive. If you plan to grow water plants, you must also consider the needs of the plants you choose. Some require deep water, while others are happier in shallow pools. The lower pool in this project is about 2½ feet (76 cm) deep. The upper pool is about 1½ feet (46 cm) deep.

Consider the future position of each pool carefully before excavating the holes. It's easier to create a true waterfall if the bank between the pools is short and steep because the water can be made to descend almost vertically. If the bank is long and only slightly sloped, the water will have to cascade over a series of stepped stones in order to reach the lower pool.

A pile of rounded river rocks, ready to be placed on the liner in a pool

These flat fieldstones will cap the rim of the pool.

To build the rim, first place a layer of soil about 6 inches (15 cm) deep around the hole. Then pack the soil down with a manually operated tamper, flaring it outward and away from the excavated hole. The rim should round over and slope gradually down on the outside; the mounded soil will stretch over the outer boundary of the sod-stripped band around your site. Continue excavating and building up the rim in this manner, tamping each layer down well, until the hole is the desired depth. The tamping will prevent later settling of the soil and shifting of the stones.

Next, at the very bottom of the hole, dig another hole a little larger than a 5-gallon (19 l) bucket. This depression will serve as a sediment catch basin. When you empty the pool to clean it out, the sediment that you hose down from the rocks and liner will be easy to remove from this central location.

Six inches (15 cm) below the water line, on the inside of the hole, cut an 8-inch-wide (20-cm) shelf into the packed soil rim, right around its circumference.

Make sure the shelf is level around its entire circumference by checking it with a string line level (a string with a very small level hooked over it). The soil and liner beneath this shelf will be covered with rounded river rocks; the soil and liner above the shelf will be covered with flatter fieldstones.

The next step is to cut out a 6-inch-wide (15-cm) shelf around the inside wall of the hole, about 18 inches (46 cm) from the bottom. This shelf will serve as a reference point when you cover the rubber liner with rocks and will also help support the rocks. Depending on the pool depth, you may need to add more 6-inch-wide (15-cm) shelves, one for every 18 inches (46 cm) of elevation. The lower pool in this project is fairly deep, and has two.

Protruding sharp-edged objects in the soil, such as rocks and roots, might puncture the pool liner, so you must remove them all. After digging the shelves, check the site very carefully, running your bare hands over the soil to locate these objects and discarding any that you find.

Lining the Lower Pool

The liner for the lower pool must cover the hole's interior and extend about 1½ feet (46 cm) beyond the mounded rim. On the uphill side, the liner should extend to the upper pool site; it will completely overlap the nearest edge of the upper pool. To estimate the size of the liner, measure the pool site at two locations: across its width and along its length.

To measure the width, start at a point 1½ feet from the exterior edge of the rim on one side of the hole. Run your tape measure from that point, over the rim, down into the center of the hole, and up again, to a point 1½ feet out from the rim on the opposite side. (Getting help from a friend will make this job much easier.) The entire length of the tape should make contact with the soil, or your liner will be too small.

To measure the length, start by standing at the low end of the slope, with the excavated hole in front of you. As you take this measurement, your tape will run directly up the slope you're facing. Place the tape 1½ feet (46 cm) out from the exterior edge of the mounded rim. Then run the tape up over the rim, down into the hole, and up the sloped bank behind the hole, until it extends beyond the near edge of the upper pool site.

Ask a friend for help spreading the liner over the hole. Allow the center of the liner to drape down into the hole and place a few rocks on the ends to keep it from sliding back down. Then take off your shoes and slide down into the hole. Starting with the sediment catch basin, gradually work the liner against the walls of the hole, pressing it against the soil as you go. Don't worry if the material forms tucks and folds; these are inevitable. When the liner is in place, temporarily secure its edges by placing large stones on them. (You'll cut the liner to size at a later stage.)

Stones, water, and plants transform an ordinary slope into an idyllic landscape.

Setting the Stones

Before setting the rounded river rocks, rinse them off well or clinging soil will add unnecessary sediment to the pool water. Next, place a large flat rock in the bottom of the sediment catch basin and loosely fill the rest of the basin with several large stones.

Start laying out river rocks in the bottom of the lined pool. Select these carefully so they'll fit together closely and cover as much of the liner as possible. The stones must lock together well; unlike stone pavers, they won't be secured by soil or gravel. To settle the rocks, strike each one several times with a 3-pound (1.4 kg) dense rubber mallet.

Continue to set river rocks up the wall of the hole, working until you've lined the first 6-inch-wide (15-cm) shelf with rocks. From this point, your walls will begin to rise more steeply. You'll use the shelf as a base for the stones you stack as you continue upward, but first you must set the pump.

Placing the Pump

The pump should be placed on the side of the pool that is closest to your source of electricity. Attach the hose to the back of the pump and set the pump on the shelf stones. Then construct stone side walls around the pump, allowing the hose to exit from the back, and cap the stone walls off with another stone to form a safe recessed area—one from which you can retrieve the pump easily if it ever needs repairs or replacement. Run the electrical cord out the back of the pump housing, over the lined rim of the hole, to the source of electricity.

Next, run the hose along the shelf toward the rising soil bank. Bring the hose up over the mounded rim and up one side of the bank toward the upper pool. You'll bury it under the stones that you set along the edge of the waterfall.

River rocks are stacked to the uppermost shelf, which defines the future water line.

Art compacts the clay soil behind the pond liner by pounding the soil with a mallet.

After laying out the cord and hose, continue to set river rocks right up to the next shelf and then on to the 8-inch-wide (20-cm) shelf above. Use the largest river rocks available to create the last course; the upper surfaces of these rocks should be even with the shelf.

The rounded river rocks below the uppermost shelf will rest below the water line. The flat fieldstones above them will appear above water level. The hose, shown to the right, will recirculate water to the pool above.

As shown in the photo to the right, Art sets the stones on the sloped walls of the hole by pulling the liner back over the stones and pounding the soil in behind them. This creates small nodes of soil that press forward, with the liner, to fill the gaps between stones, locking the stones together.

Next, working from the shelf upward, set a few courses of fieldstones or quarried stones with two opposing flat faces, stepping the stones back in each course. The first course of flat stones should rest on the 8-inch-wide (20-cm) shelf and on the upper surfaces of the last course of river rock.

Take care not to crush the garden hose as you continue to set the flat stones in place; weave the hose through the gaps and make sure the rocks are secure, or they'll shift.

Setting a Runoff Pipe

Heavy rainfall will raise the water level in the lower pool significantly. To prevent the excess water from flooding over the rim, the pool must have an outlet. Before stacking rocks to cover the rim at the low end of the pool, pull the liner back from the mounded soil and dig out a small channel, about 8 inches (20 cm) wide and 8 inches deep. Replace the liner, tucking it into the

Flat fieldstones are stacked to form the waterfall area between the two pools.

Water from the upper pool will travel through the narrow channel shown under construction here. The electrical cord from the submersible pump appears in the upper left-hand corner. The pump itself is hidden in a carefully stacked stone niche.

channel, and position the end of a 4-inch-diameter (10 cm) non-perforated pipe on top of the liner. The open end of the pipe should sit back in the channel rather than hanging out over the pool and should rest at a height that will allow excess water to drain through it.

Now grasp the liner on the inside wall of the pool and tuck it loosely into the open end of the pipe, just around its rim. (You'll have to fold the liner to do this.) Then line the channel walls in front of the pipe with small flat stones, flaring them outward at the end of the channel so they'll funnel excess water into the pipe.

Bury the end of the excess pipe in a trench or simply leave it short and open so that the runoff will flow directly out of the pool and into the soil.

Finishing up the Lower Pool

Continue dry-stacking stones up to the top of the mounded rim. Next, at the lower end of the pool, use a utility knife to trim the liner back to the rim's outer edge. Bury the remaining liner in the soil at the outer edge of the stonework. Then cover the rest of the rim with dry-stacked stones.

Cover the lined, sloped bank at the uphill end of the pool with dry-stacked stones, weaving the garden hose in behind them, along one side, so you can position it in the upper pool. As you can see in the photo above, in order to support the waterfall stone, Art placed a very large vertical stone against the lined bank, setting it at a slight angle.

A careful stone arrangement sends splashing water into the lower pool.

The level shown in the photo on the previous page is placed in the half-built spillway, which leads from the site of the upper pool, out to the waterfall stone. Arrange your stones to create a similar channel.

The way in which you position the stones will determine how the water descends from one pool to the other. A very long, horizontally positioned waterfall stone will direct water out and then straight down; the water won't contact the stones in the bank as it descends. A shorter waterfall stone or one set farther back will allow water to cascade over other stones. After you've tested the flow of water, you'll almost certainly have to reposition some of these stones.

With a bucket of water or a garden hose, check the position of the spillway stones by directing water over them. Adjust the stones as necessary. If your waterfall will cascade over other stones, position these stones to avoid excessive splashing, as splashing water evaporates quickly.

A waterfall garden brings the splendid sight and tranquil sound of falling water close to home.

Creating the Upper Pool

To excavate the upper pool, first pull back the liner that extends up from the lower pool. Then dig a hole, sediment catch basin, and shelves as before and bring the liner back over the front rim of the new hole. Measure and cut a second liner to size and cover the new hole with it, overlapping the first liner as you do.

Bring the pump hose to the uphill side of the second pool and position its outflow end about 1 inch (2.5 cm) below the desired water level. Then cover the liner in and around the upper pool with stacked stones. If your upper pool is considerably smaller than the lower one, use smaller river rocks to line it below the water line.

Pool Maintenance

Check the water levels in your pools frequently and add more water as necessary. You'd be surprised by how quickly water can evaporate, especially during hot, dry weather. Periodically, use a skimming net to scoop leaves from the water and a garden rake to scrape them from the bottom of each pool. To clean the pools, first siphon the water out and hose down the rocks. Then scoop the accumulated sediment and debris from the catch basins and refill the pools with fresh water.

CHAPTER EIGHT

STEPS, TERRACES, BENCHES, AND BORDERS

If your land is completely flat, you may want to skip right to the section on benches at the end of this chapter. Stone benches make lovely additions to any outdoor setting, and although the stones used to build them are heavy, their construction is remarkably easy.

If your land includes a sloped area, the first few projects are bound to please you. Dry-laid steps and dry-stacked walls for terraced areas provide practical and attractive ways to prevent erosion, turn slopes into garden beds, and avoid sliding down muddy hillsides on your way to the chicken coop.

Dry-laid stone steps go hand-in-hand with steep terraced slopes, as they provide easy access to the planting beds behind the terraced walls.

Dry-Laid Steps

Stone steps, formal or informal, not only serve a practical purpose, but also provide decorative focal points in
garden landscapes. Steps and paths should always be your
first considerations as you lay out an overall landscape
design, so select these sites before establishing sites for
walls, garden beds, benches, and stone sculptures.

Treads and Risers

The *tread* of a step is the surface you step on; its
depth is the measurement from its front to its back. The
riser is the vertical front portion. To make sure your steps
are easy to negotiate, the depth of the tread and height
of the riser (a dimension known as the *rise*) should be
consistent from step to step. This is especially important

when the steps are located in a high-use area such as the front entrance of your home. If the rise of one step is 4 inches (10 cm), for example, the rise of every other step should be as close to 4 inches as possible. Why? Consistency in these dimensions creates the sense of predictability that keeps us from stumbling as we go up and down a flight of steps.

The rise of an outdoor step should be between 4 and 8 inches (10 and 20 cm), although free-form steps for private use may be 10 or more inches (25 cm) tall. The standard building code for indoor steps is 7 ¼ inches (18.4 cm). Tread depths usually range from 10 to 18 inches (25 to 46 cm). The relationship between riser and tread dimensions will vary from one set of steps to another, of course. Steps on a long gradual slope, for example, may have fairly deep treads and fairly short risers, while a steep slope may require narrow treads and tall risers.

Following is one of the best formulas for determining a suitable tread depth and rise:

(Rise x 2) + tread depth = 26 inches (66 cm)

If, for example, you want a 5-inch-tall (13-cm) riser, your tread depth should be 16 inches (41 cm).

Overall Rise and Run

The horizontal distance covered by a series of steps is known as the *run*. This measurement is taken along an imaginary, level, horizontal line. The overall rise of a series of steps is a measurement taken along a plumb, vertical line.

Deciding how many steps you'll need for a given slope requires calculating the rise and run of your sloped site. As you learn how to do this, remember that because stones differ in size and surface area, the dimensions of each step won't always be exact. If your steps are meeting up to a fixed point, such as a patio or a paved

Boulders help lock these steps into place.

pathway, this measurement will be critical. On the other hand, if the spot where the steps begin and end is arbitrary, this measurement is less important.

The easiest way to measure the rise and run at your own step site is with the help of a friend. You'll need two 2×4s, one at least 8 feet (2.4 m) long; a couple of 2- to 4-foot-long (0.6- to 1.2-m) levels; a measuring tape; and a pencil.

To mark the ground where you'd like the top and bottom steps to be, pound in a stake at each location. Then give your friend a level, a 2×4, and the pencil. Have your friend hold the 2×4 upright next to the bottom stake, checking it for plumb with the level. Take the other 2×4 (the longer one) and position it horizontally, with one end at the upper stake. Check its position with a level as well. The two 2×4s should meet at a 90-degree angle. The lower edge of the horizontal 2×4 represents the run of the steps; the inner edge of the vertical 2×4 represents the rise (figure 1).

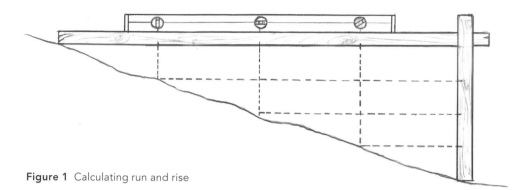

Figure 1 Calculating run and rise

Next, have your friend make a pencil mark on each 2 × 4, at the inside corner where the two pieces of lumber meet. After making these marks, place the 2 × 4s on the ground and measure the marked distance on each one. These two measurements constitute the rise and run of your future steps.

After calculating the rise and run of the slope, you can use the results to come up with tread depths and riser heights to suit your site. For example, if the run of your site is 6 feet (183 cm) and you'd like to have four steps, divide 6 feet by 4 to get the depth of each tread—in this case, 18 inches (46 cm). To calculate the rise of each step, divide the overall rise of the slope by 4; the result is 4 inches (10 cm).

With dry-laid stone steps, it's difficult to keep riser heights and tread depths consistent, but do try to stay within ½-inch (13 mm) of your riser dimension and within 1 inch (2.5 cm) of your estimated tread dimension.

Let me offer two tips here. First, if the run of your step site is exceptionally long, consider incorporating one or more landings. A landing provides space for two people to pass in a series of steps and may be a welcome spot for people to stop to catch their breath. If your steps are narrow, landings also provide "passing" places when someone climbing the steps meets someone on their way down. Landings can consist of small paved areas, level areas of lawn, or border-contained gravel beds. (When you calculate the number of steps you'll need for your slope, just treat the landing as if it were a step.) It'll be easier to incorporate a landing in an area where the slope is less severe. The bottom landing can be the ground or the end of a path.

Second, a few slopes are just too steep to be suitable for steps. Their run is so short and their rise so tall, that the step treads would be too shallow and the risers too tall to negotiate safely. One way to handle a steep slope is to angle the steps across it; this will increase the run and decrease the rise for each step.

Step Width

The ideal step is 4 to 5 feet (1.2 to 1.5 m) wide and allows two people to walk comfortably side by side. If your steps will serve only as a functional route from one place to another, a more practical width is 2 to 3 feet (61 to 76 cm). Unlike riser heights and tread depths, the width of each step, from end to end, isn't as critical. This is fortunate, as existing landscape features such as trees sometimes make it impossible to set treads that are equal in width. Consider varying step widths even if other features aren't in the way. A flight of steps that is wide at the bottom and narrow at the top can have a wonderful visual effect.

Selecting Stone

Large, heavy pieces of stone work best for this type of project. Use a medium to dense stone, as soft stones will wear out too quickly. Sandstone works well for general use in most house and garden settings. Basalt, slate, gneiss, or quarried granite will also work. The granite steps up to the Capitol building in Washington, D.C., are used daily by thousands of people. With that type of daily use, granite is about the only stone that can hold up from one decade to the next. Granite, however, is extremely heavy and much harder to shape than other stones.

The flagstone used in the project beginning on this page is light gray sandstone of medium density quarried along the Cumberland Plateau in Eastern Tennessee. In Pennsylvania, along the Delaware River, a similar stone is quarried and referred to as blue stone because of its blue-green color. In the southwestern United States, flagstone comes in a variety of earth tones from brown and tan to pink and red.

It's common to find this type of stone precut for steps, paving, and mantels. Special orders are not unusual, but they can take four to six weeks for delivery. This type of stone is sold by the square foot when cut to specific dimensions and by weight with more random shapes.

Steps, a short pathway, and low walls transform a bank into a welcoming site. Low-level lighting makes the steps safe at night.

Dry-Laid Steps with Built-Up Risers

Formal-looking steps have consistent riser heights and tread depths, and the stones that act as treads are supported by separate riser stones.

Selecting Stones

Stones similar to the ones you'd use as capstones for dry-stacked retaining walls, each about 2 to 4 inches (5 to 10 cm) thick, offer good tread surfaces. Look for stones with surfaces that are fairly even and coarse-textured. (Very smooth stones won't provide a good grip when they're wet.) Check these stones for any protrusions on their front edges. If you find any, trim them away, as they may trip people using the steps. If the stones you use as treads aren't equal in thickness, you can make up for the differences by using riser stones of different heights.

Site Preparation

If possible, place your stones at the top of the step site, not at the bottom of the bank. Sliding stones down the bank and into place is much easier than dragging them uphill. Also be sure to have a large tarp on hand for covering the site if it rains. If you want to add lighting along the edges of the steps, bring the light fixtures and cables to your site as well. As you set the stones, you'll bury the cables to one side of the steps.

Begin by removing the sod from the entire site. Next, excavate a 4-inch-deep (10-cm) trench, from the top of the site to the bottom. Dig this trench 6 inches (15 cm) wider on each side than your steps will be; this will give you some working space and, if your slope is very steep, will also leave room for the additional stones you must set in order to retain exposed soil. Then make rough cuts for every step, removing the bulk of the soil from each spot where a tread will rest.

Another way to build stone steps is to strip the sod and dig out the areas for the steps one at a time, setting stones in the cut before excavating for the step above it. If you choose this method, spread a small tarp over each

After setting the riser stones, lower the tread stone into place with its front edge (the nose) overhanging the riser stones by about 1 inch (2.5 cm). The packed gravel bed offers a solid, well-drained surface for the back of the tread to rest on securely.

tread after setting it in order to keep it clear of soil as you excavate the next spot. Each time you're ready to move the tarp, slide it off the step it covers and shake any loose soil from it.

Setting the First Tread

At the bottom of the site, excavate a level area a little larger than the bottom of your first tread. (You may set this tread so either its top or bottom surface is at ground level.) Shovel the soil into a wheelbarrow and cart it to a nearby spot. You may need this soil to dress out the site when you're finished.

Next, spread a 2-inch-thick (5-cm) bed of gravel over the level area. Then position one or more stones on the gravel, pitching them slightly downward from back to front to help them shed water. This is a good place to use a stone with a very large surface area, although any tread may be made up of more than one stone. If you use two or more stones, be sure their front edges meet one another as closely as possible at the joint or joints.

Digging into the bank for the next step

Small pieces of select stone are carefully stacked and leveled to construct the risers.

Check to see that the upper surfaces are even and that the tread surface is level from side to side. (Humps and depressions in many stones make it difficult to level them exactly, so don't be too picky.) The stones must be secure; treads that wobble are unsafe as well as annoying.

Setting the First Riser

For maximum stability, the riser stone (or stones) for the next step should be placed on the back edge of the tread beneath. If the tread you've set isn't deep enough to allow a riser stone to rest on it, compensate by placing another thick stone behind the tread, one large enough to make up the difference in tread depth as well as support the riser above it. Dig out some soil at the back edge of the tread and add 2 inches (5 cm) of gravel to this area (figure 2). Then place the additional stone on this bed and pack additional gravel around it.

Riser stones retain the gravel on the step sites behind them and support the treads above them. To figure out

Figure 2 Packed gravel supports the tread stone.

how tall a given riser stone must be, first measure the thickness of the tread that will be placed above it. Subtract this tread thickness from the desired rise measurement you selected when you first designed your steps. If, for example, you want the rise of each step to be 8 inches (20 cm), and the tread thickness is 3 inches (8 cm), your riser stone should be 5 inches (13 cm) tall. You may use more than one riser stone to achieve this height; just stack them on top of one another.

Building up the first riser and backfilling with gravel

Exposed areas along the sides of the steps need to be plugged with stones in order to retain the gravel backfill.

Work Your Way Up

I once had a man ask me for advice on building stone steps. He'd already started his project but was so frustrated he was ready to give up. I started to share some tips on moving the stones and where to start work, when he stopped me, grinning with embarrassment. After a moment, he explained that he'd started building his steps by setting the top one first and was now trying to work his way down.

When you're building steps, always work from the bottom up. Because stone steps usually overlap one another, working downhill is an almost impossible task. Starting at the bottom also provides you with a series of convenient work areas as you move up the slope.

Position the riser stone or stones on top of the back edge of the tread stone that you've already set. Then backfill the space between the riser and the soil behind it with gravel. To keep the backfill from migrating out from behind the riser, you must also set stones at its ends, as if you were creating a corner on a retaining wall. After setting these stones, tamp the gravel backfill, being careful not to shift the stones.

Finishing the Steps

Spread a gravel bed for the next tread. Then brush away all gravel from the top edge of the built-up riser. Set the tread in place; its front end must rest on the riser beneath so that it is well supported. Either set the front edge of the tread flush with the face of the riser or allow it to overlap the riser by up to 1 inch (2.5 cm). If you allow too much overhang, the tread will be difficult to stabilize.

Continue setting risers and treads in this fashion until you reach the top of your site. If you're using more than one stone to make up each riser and tread, your steps will be more attractive if you alternate the joints, so they don't fall along a single line from one step to another (figure 3).

You may find that you need to retain exposed soil along the sides of your steps. On gradual slopes, stand large stones on edge, as shown to the right, leaning them toward the exposed soil. On steeper slopes, use chunky, irregularly shaped stones.

Adding extra stones along the sides of steps will also provide visual anchors for step corners that jut out sharply from the soil bank. To create a border effect, position these stones so they rise above the upper surfaces of the treads.

In a run of steps, the risers and tread stones can vary considerably in thickness.

Stone Slab Steps

Formal stone steps may also be built without using any riser stones. Instead, a very thick slab serves as the tread and riser for each step. The front edge of each stone overlaps the back edge of the one beneath it.

Selecting Stones

For this step-building method, use large stones, each as thick as the rise measurement you chose after calculating the overall rise and run of your site. If you want the rise of each step to be 4 inches (10 cm), for example, each stone should be close to 4 inches thick.

Most stones appropriate for this style of step-building weigh in excess of 150 pounds (68 kg). Although the simple engineering tricks provided on pages 22–25

Figure 3 Vary the positions of the joints between tread stones from one step to the next and use chunky stones to retain exposed soil.

The consistent thickness of these carefully selected stone slabs eliminated the need for built-up risers.

make it possible for one person to move very heavy slabs, unless you can place these stones at the top of your site and slide them downhill as you work, consider making steps with built-up risers and thinner tread stones instead.

If your site is steep, the stones may need to be as thick as 8 inches (20 cm) and may be relatively short from front to back. Your goal, as you construct these steps, is to keep variations in rise and tread depth to within ½ inch (13 mm) and 1 inch (2.5 cm) respectively.

If your stones vary in thickness, add shim stones as needed. You don't need to make every finished tread the same width from one side to the other. Instead, use plants or chunky stones to fill any gaps at the ends.

Setting the First Stone

Select the stone or stones for the first step. If you use several stones to make this first tread, be sure their meeting edges match well.

Slide the stone or stones down to the base of the site. Excavate an area for the first step, making it slightly larger than the surface area of the stone or stones. Spreading a 2-inch-thick (5 cm) bed of gravel is optional with very large stones; their weight will prevent them from shifting. A gravel base, however, does make minor adjustments easier.

Set the first stone or stones in place, pitching the step slightly downward from back to front and checking it for level from side to side. Then use a metal rod to pack gravel around its edges or, if you're using rock dust or soil, a rubber mallet. To retain the soil along the outer edges, set chunks of stone as needed.

Spread a small tarp across the step you've just set and prepare a level site for the second step, right behind the first one. Before you excavate the soil from the bank, select a stone for this step and measure its depth so you don't cut too far back into the bank. If you want this next step to sit on a bed of gravel, dig this area 2 inches (5 cm) deeper than the upper surface of the first step and then spread out the gravel bed. If you've decided to set your stones without gravel beds, excavate this spot to make the soil level with the upper surface of the first step.

Because the second step will overlap the first one, you must also mark the first tread where you want the front edge of the second step to sit. Use a tape measure to measure off the desired tread depth on the first step

Located at the North Carolina Arboretum in Asheville, North Carolina, these
steps include shim stones to keep the rise consistent from step to step.

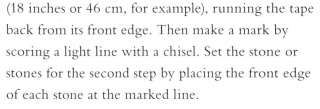

Stonemason Frederica Lashley selected large stones with wide, even surfaces so that the steps she built would be easy to negotiate in spite of their variations in height.

Unusually tall risers were used to navigate a steep bank.

(18 inches or 46 cm, for example), running the tape back from its front edge. Then make a mark by scoring a light line with a chisel. Set the stone or stones for the second step by placing the front edge of each stone at the marked line.

Check the second step for level and pitch; then continue setting stones until the steps have been completed.

Free-Form Steps

The free-form steps described in this section are the easiest and quickest stone steps to build because you can use a wide variety of stones rather than carefully selected stone slabs. You must use large, heavy stones, but they don't need to be perfectly shaped; climbing informal free-form steps can sometimes be almost like climbing boulders! You may also incorporate other materials, such as short logs.

The steps shown in the photo on the facing page extend down a steep bank, at the base of which are a creek and small dam. The dam serves as the water intake for a small micro-hydroelectric unit, so silt from the creek must be removed from the dam from time to time. The silt is shoveled into perforated containers, allowed to drain, and then carried up the bank and used as a garden soil amendment. Before I built these steps, the damp, bare, shady bank was quite difficult to negotiate. Fortunately, I was able to place my materials at the top of this site, so I didn't have to drag the stones up the bank as I worked.

When I designed these steps, function was my primary consideration, as the site isn't very visible, and the steps aren't used by the general public. The steep, short bank required unusually tall risers. None of the risers or treads are the same size.

As you can see in the photo, the first step is supported by the dam and by small stones that I pulled from the creek and placed to one side of the dam. Figures 4 through 6 show the various stages of building these steps. (Note that the dam doesn't appear in these illustrations.)

First, I made the cuts in the bank with a short-handled digging spade (figure 4). Because my stones were so large and heavy, I didn't need to spread gravel beds for them, but if you use smaller stones, be sure to set them in gravel. I slid the first stone down the bank, leaving the remaining stones at the top and out of the way.

After setting the first stone securely, I rolled a large, block-shaped stone into place to serve as the next tread. Then, to prevent the exposed soil at its ends from spreading across the surfaces of the steps, I set irregularly shaped, chunky stones in place along the edges (figure 5).

The third step required some shimming along its front edge. To support the front edge of the last stone, I placed a long stone on its narrow edge, sinking that edge 4 inches (10 cm) deep in the ground (figure 6).

Figure 4

Figure 5

Figure 6

Set in a remote area of Grandfather Mountain, in North Carolina, these
free-form stone steps were made with large stones found nearby.

Locust-Log-and-Stone Steps

I built the serpentine steps shown here with a combination of large stones and locust logs. Because I didn't have any help on this project, I relied heavily on my pry bar, a few wide locust boards, and the force of gravity.

At the top of the slope, I was able to unload enough stones from my truck to build the upper three-quarters of the steps. One by one, I slid the huge stones to the edge of the tailgate and then flipped them over onto the ground. (A bed liner in the back of your truck will make this job infinitely easier.) After each stone hit the ground, I moved it off to one side, so the next stone wouldn't land on top of it.

To build the first few steps, I used locust logs, placing each one on a bed of gravel. To stabilize the logs, I pounded large locust stakes into the soil in front of them. To create the flat tread area on each log, I used a chainsaw to cut a series of kerfs and then removed the excess wood with a hammer and chisel.

I chose a stone for the next step and excavated a place for it. To move the stone down from the top of the site, I arranged wide locust boards end to end, down the bank, to a point just above the locust-log steps. Next, I walked the stone, on its edges, over to the top board. I set the stone down flat on the board and slid it halfway down. Then I moved to the downhill side of the stone and supported it while tugging and sliding it down over the boards. (At times, I had to hold the stone back to keep it from moving down the boards too quickly.)

To distribute the weight of extremely thick stones, I placed another board next to the one already in place to provide extra support. When the stone I was moving reached the bottom end of the paired boards, I moved the extra board and placed it by the next board down. Sometimes, a stone would start to shift off the two boards; I used a pry bar to shove it back into place.

A narrow set of steps is easily built into this dry-stacked retaining wall of lichen-covered stones.

Building Steps into a Wall

To build steps into a wall, figure exactly where you want them to be positioned before you start laying the wall's foundation course. Often a series of steps looks more interesting when it starts out wider at the bottom and narrows slightly as the steps reach the top.

Integrate the stone steps with the retaining wall by building the two elements at the same time. Refer to page 51 for more information on retaining walls.

When you're at the point of laying out the wall's foundation, make the steps the priority by setting your landing stone(s) and first step. Then set the wall's foundation course and any additional courses needed to meet up level with the surface of the first tread. Set cornerstones and wall ends on both sides of the step's opening.

Backfill behind the wall's first course, set your next step, and then continue bringing the wall up even with the surface of the second step. Once the second step is set, you'll see that the steps are passing through the wall. Set wall end stones running perpendicular to the length of the wall's face so they run back into the bank of soil. The stonework at the wall end will be capped off and stepped upward along with the treads and risers.

Retaining Walls for Terraces

For centuries, people around the world, from Italy to Asia and South America, have cut terraces into sloped land and buttressed the soil banks with dry-stacked retaining walls. These walls transformed steep slopes into arable land, protected hillside towns and temples, and even served as seats in amphitheaters.

In today's gardens, terraced walls are usually built to provide level areas for planting and to make steep slopes more accessible and attractive. Separating a slope into narrow terraces by building several short retaining walls, one above the other, offers a more attractive result than building very tall retaining walls with huge stones. Low stone walls are also much easier to stack; lifting large stones above shoulder height or working from scaffolding is difficult!

Creative combinations of materials such as locust logs and stones can provide wonderful effects. I've even seen a terrace supported by an 8-foot-tall (2.4 m) retaining wall made with used tires—and the wall looked charming! The overlapped tires were stepped gradually back into the bank behind them; the exposed holes in them were filled with soil and planted with wildflowers. Large slabs of recycled concrete walkway also make good dry-stacking material. Treated landscape timbers and railroad ties are practical choices, but walls built with them often lack visual appeal.

Depending on how steep your site is, and the visual impact you wish to make, terraced retaining walls can take any number of shapes. The photos in this section depict just a few of the many design possibilities.

Before sketching your terrace design or excavating the site, calculate the rise and run of the slope, using the method described on pages 177–178. (If you have access to a surveyor's transit and know how to use it, by all means do!) Then figure out the location of each retaining wall as if the wall itself were a step riser and the bed behind it were a tread.

Always start at the bottom of the slope. If you're having stones delivered from a stone yard, ask the driver to leave only enough stone there to build the first wall. Set the remaining stones at the top of the slope. If you can't get your materials to the top of the site, enlist some friends or hire someone to help.

Built with stone, gravel, and soil, these terraced walls along the Cinque Terra of northern Italy are more than seven centuries old.

Rising up from the Mediterranean coast, these terraced walls were built 8 to 10 feet (2.4 to 3 m) tall in order to provide strips of level soil 4 to 5 feet (1.2 to 1.5 m) wide.

The soil behind terraced walls doesn't have to be perfectly
level. These slightly sloped beds are perfect for planting.

My neighbor Jackie Taylor combined stones and locust
logs to create garden beds in her backyard.

Stone Benches

Imagine taking a welcome rest and enjoying your favorite vista while you sit on a bench you've built yourself. A well-built stone bench, set in a favorite location, will see years of use and will require little or no maintenance.

Freestanding Benches

Freestanding benches—the simplest kind to build— may be located almost anywhere: under a tree, in the middle of a garden, on a woodland path, or next to a playground.

Although stone benches may not be as comfortable as garden furniture, when they're set in the right location, they're just as inviting. Choose a site to which you've always been drawn. A bench set in an area that you rarely visit won't get the use it deserves.

The size of your bench stone (the stone you'll sit on) will determine how difficult it is to set. Some of the benches shown in this section were built by a single person, but help from a friend always makes setting these heavy stones easier.

Selecting Stone

The hardest part in building a freestanding bench will be finding a slab 3 to 5 feet (.9 to 1.5 m) long and the supporting stones. If you're not lucky enough to have an old piece of granite curbstone lying around, a trip to the stone yard may be in order. Don't count on finding exactly what you're looking for the first visit. Let people there know what you're looking for, and they may be willing to keep an eye out for you. Bench stones don't have to be rectangular in shape, but they should be heavy and at least 2 inches (5.1 cm) thick.

The oddly shaped supports of this playful-looking bench nevertheless provide a stable base for the bench stone.

This massive stone slab conceals the supporting stones, giving the impression that the bench is floating.

Large slabs of quarried stone were used to build this freestanding table.

A cornerstone from an abandoned foundation was used to make this stunning bench.

Climbing vines lend old-world charm to this dry-stacked bench.

Triangular, rounded, and squared slabs of stone will also work, although they'll require three or four supports.

A bench stone should have a fairly even top surface, free of major protrusions that would be uncomfortable to sit on. If the bench stone's underside is also even, it'll make better contact with the top of the support stones. For narrow rectangular benches, each of the two supporting stones should be blocky with enough surface area on one of their ends to amply cover the width of the slab. When three or more stones support a bench, it's less critical how much surface area comes into contact underneath the slab. Rounded stones with just a small point of contact work well when three or more support stones are used. The contact points of the stones will need to be of even height for the bench to sit level.

One way to support a bench stone is to place two substantial stones underneath it. As you calculate the required height of these two stones, keep three facts in mind. First, a comfortable height for the upper surface of a bench is 16 to 18 inches (41 to 46 cm). Second, you'll set the two supporting stones about 4 to 6 inches (10 to 15 cm) deep in the soil—and even deeper if they're especially narrow. Third, you must include the thickness of the bench stone as you estimate the overall height of the bench.

Let's consider an example. You've decided that you want your bench to be 17 inches (43 cm) tall. Your bench stone is 4 inches thick, so you subtract 4 inches from 17 inches to get 13 inches (33 cm). Your supporting stones will be set 5 inches (13 cm) deep in the ground, so you add 5 inches to 13 inches. The height of each supporting stone should therefore be 18 inches (46 cm).

This simple stone bench is a great place to greet the morning sun.

The backrest stone of this bench was sunk into an earthen socket dug well below ground level.

A single stone serves as a backrest for this retaining-wall bench.

Look for supporting stones that are close to equal height. (You may compensate for minor differences by sinking the taller stone further into the ground.) The tops should be fairly flat and even, so they'll make good contact with the bench stone, and the bottoms must sit securely in the soil.

When you're ready to build the bench, start by measuring the length of the bench stone. Next, set the supporting stones so the bench stone will overlap them by 6 to 8 inches (15 to 20 cm) at each end. Make sure the tops of the supporting stones are level. Then set the bench stone. If this stone is heavier at one end than at the other, allowing the lighter end to overlap its supporting stone by a greater length makes the bench appear more balanced.

Another way to support a bench stone is to stack stones horizontally beneath it. If the ground is firm, dig a shallow, level spot for the first stone. In soft, loamy soil, excavate an area large enough to hold both the first stone and a 4-inch-thick (10 cm) bed of gravel underneath it. Tamp the gravel into the excavated area, set the first stone, and tamp more gravel around it. Check the stone for level; then continue dry-stacking stones to build the support. Two to three large stones look better in these kinds of supports than several smaller stones. Try to use large stones that fit together tightly. If you need to use smaller chinking or shim stones to steady the bench stone, place them in the least visible areas. A bench stone that rocks even slightly is very bothersome. Whether you're working alone or have the help of a friend, take care to adjust this stone carefully on its supports. To find the best possible position, you may need to slide the bench stone back and forth across the supports until it's stable.

Retaining Wall Benches

A bench may also be built right into a dry-stacked retaining wall. The portion of the wall that serves as the bench should be 16 to 18 inches (41 to 46 cm) in height. The simplest way to build a backrest for this kind of bench is to set large stones on edge, leaning them back against the soil bank at any angle that's comfortable for you.

A backrest may also be dry-stacked as a part of the retaining wall. To do this, you must cut back into the soil bank in order to accommodate the backrest stones. You must also tie the backrest stones into the wall stones at the back corners of the bench and set capstones at its top. Whether you stack them as part of the wall or set them separately, backrest stones should rest on the back edges of the bench stones, about 18 inches (46 cm) from the front of the bench.

The bench at the corner of this wall includes a raised ledge that makes a fine armrest.

CHAPTER NINE

STONE EXPRESSIONS

Every time we dry-stack a wall or build a stone sculpture, we join the thousands of people before us who have expressed themselves in stone. Magnificent Incan temples, humble Viking hearths, Egyptian pyramids, Stone-Age Druid burial sites, and simple stone walls in pastures all give voice to an essential aspect of our lives: our need for shelter, for permanence, for spirituality, and for beauty.

■ MATT GODDARD

A serpentine retaining wall built of basalt, argillite, rhyolite, and sandstone. Skillfully hewn basalt stones top the wall and provide sharp contrast to the lighter-colored rock throughout.

At the end of the wall are limestone slab steps and hefty basalt columns. Colorful river rock allows for drainage and echoes the many colors of the wall.

■ MATT GODDARD

An up-close look at the intricately fitted stones. Niches in the rock design provide places for candles.

■ MARC ARCHAMBAULT

Small pieces of a locally quarried metamorphic stone surround colorful Pennsylvania stone in this path. Mexican beach pebbles, orthoceras, and ammonite fossils are tucked into the joinery, rewarding closer inspection.

■ MARC ARCHAMBAULT

Several types of stone were used in order to accent the color and texture in this stone mosaic patio. Commissioned and owned by the City of Gainesville, Florida, the design was inspired by the fossil-rich limestone of the state. Upon close observation, a nautilus shape will emerge to the eye, while the intersecting lines suggest the movement of water.

■ MATT GODDARD

Mortared sandstone pieces in bold hues were strategically positioned next to one another to produce a vivid visual contrast. The walkway is lined with reclaimed granite cobbles.

■ CHUCK EBLACKER

A dry-stone settee is the focal point in this bluestone patio. Vertically set stone cleverly placed in descending height forms a pleasing arch in the backrest of the seat.

■ CHUCK EBLACKER

Vertically laid stone suspends a boulder, making an intriguing focal point for this outer garden room dry-stone wall.

DAVID FINDLAY WILSON

The vertical placement of the Cotswold Limestone provides an attractive visual backdrop for the flowers growing among this dry-stacked wall built for the Salisbury Hospital Rehabilitation Garden for Spinal Unit.

JOE DINWIDDIE

An oak stump makes a sturdy base and elevates this stone structure above the forest undergrowth. The design is loosely based on the style of stone figures in the Arctic region, called Inuksuk, but this sculpture is in Brevard, North Carolina.

DAVID FINDLAY WILSON

Intricate herringbone design stone walls over 437 yards (400 m) in length greet travelers at the Edinburgh Airport Interchange in Scotland.

■ CHUCK EBLACKER

The dry stone walls and fire pit are capped with heavy bluestone, providing a nice frame for this patio. The low wall is at a perfect height for sitting, so there's ample seating to enjoy the fire pit.

■ JASON HOFFMAN

This free-standing dry-stone wall built with sandstone is located in Dunblane, Scotland. The curved portion of the wall makes a tight 100-degree turn.

■ CHUCK EBLACKER

This pizza oven is a testament to well fitted stone as is exemplified in the arches and the overall pleasing shape of structure. A masonry backing was used in the construction.

■ ALAN ASH

Large boulders bookend a free-standing dry-stone river-rock wall.

■ JASON HOFFMAN

This undulating wall was built around an orchard in Collessie, Scotland. Scottish shoot butts—stone circles built into earth banks and used by hunters to shoot game birds—inspired the design. The turf top is a traditional "West of Scotland" method of completing walls, particularly where there is a dearth of good coping stones. None of the 200-foot wall is straight.

■ JOE DINWIDDIE

The color variations in the Tennessee Crab Orchard sandstone makes for a visually striking walkway.

■ JOE DINWIDDIE

Located in western Pennsylvania, this fence was built from locally salvaged sandstone—700 tons of it. It took six years of intermittent work to complete the fence and retaining wall around the original stagecoach stop in the town of Armagh.

■ CHUCK EBLACKER

Interspersed along the dry-stone walkway and patio, small river stones were inverted and then placed face-down to form patterns. The dry-stone recycled Medina sandstone steps are 4 to 5 inches thick and held in place by gravity and friction.

■ JOE DINWIDDIE

This fire pit, bench, and patio arrangement is located in Black Mountain, North Carolina, and was designed by local landscape architect, Greg Cloos. The bench and patio stones are Crab Orchard sandstone from Tennessee, and the fire pit is ringed with firebrick.

■ CHUCK EBLACKER

This moongate is a testament to the power and strength of dry stone. Only gravity and friction hold the arch and walls together. Small nooks add interest, and step stiles protruding from the wall provide an alternative exit over the top.

An internal view of the moongate, now planted with greenery.

■ CHUCK EBLACKER

Bluestone slabs are overlapped by each other and by the adjoining walls. Mortar is not needed as this technique not only ties the steps together but results in strong construction. The walls are dry laid, capped with heavy copestones laid vertically, and then topped with fitted round cobbles.

■ MATT GODDARD

This mortared patio's shape is organic and without hard lines, blending harmoniously with the arching rows of reclaimed granite cobbles.

■ JOE DINWIDDIE

This retaining wall was made from two types of salvaged stone in western Pennsylvania. The style, with the vertical copes, is similar to that found in Great Britain and central Kentucky.

■ ALAN ASH

A dry stone pillar, complete with light, attractively displays a house number.

BEFORE AND AFTER

Mark Jurus

■ BEFORE

■ AFTER

This original wall was built in 1969 with mortar and field stone from the property and is located in Glenville, Pennsylvania. The wall failed due to an underground drainpipe improperly installed within the last 10 years. The pipe leaked water into the earth behind the wall and over time, the wall was pushed over due to the hydraulic pressure. All the old stone was hauled away.

The client was interested in replacing the wall to fit the era of the home, which was built in 1813. The new wall was built using the same design as the old one, and the stones are repurposed from an old corn-crib foundation located on the property. The six large stone steps are embedded into the ground.

■ BEFORE

■ AFTER

Located in Baltimore, Maryland, the original structure was a dry-laid stone retaining wall using local stone from the site and seven mortared steps within the wall. Failure of the original construction was caused by an uprooted Beech tree from a storm. All the stone and mortar were repurposed into the new wall.

The walls and steps were rebuilt completely without mortar, using Butler stone and a mix of Pennsylvania Bluestone. The structure is 3 feet high and 10 feet long with a 16-foot-long retaining wall. The eight steps have 14-inch treads with a 6-inch rise between each. The stairway walls were built with a 1:6 batter.

■ AFTER

The new retaining wall includes a rain gutter at the back to catch water coming off the carport. The steps were made to size from slabs of Pennsylvania Bluestone using feather and wedges. Flat capstones top the wall. Since the structure was built to meet the top of the driveway, the biggest challenges were beginning the build at the bottom to hit exactly at the top of the driveway and keeping the steps and walls square.

■ BEFORE

■ AFTER

This 40-year-old railroad-tie retaining wall in Millers, Maryland, was failing due to rot.

The railroad-tie retaining wall was replaced with a 25 x 5.5 foot wall built with dry-stacked Butler stone; note the curved portion on the end. The original wooden support column was replaced with stone, eliminating any future rotting issues. Three steps now lead to the upper porch.

■ BEFORE

This original historic wall was more than 100 years old and 100 feet in length. It's in Cockeysville, Maryland, and over the years, with a new addition to the home and the addition of a blacktop driveway, the wall became smaller and smaller.

■ AFTER

The portion of the wall closest to the house was not rebuilt, just repaired. The new and old retaining walls measure 34 x 7 feet. Two rows of staggered protruding tie stones placed in the wall help to tie together the front and back walls in addition to lending support as the wall settles over time.

■ AFTER

The original wall had an almost vertical batter. In this photo you can see the beauty of the curved portion with its 1:8 batter. The capstones were designed to overhang a couple of inches to provide a pleasing visual contrast.

■ AFTER

The steps were constructed to give the illusion of floating. The biggest challenge was building the steps into the curved wall. Each step was made to size from slabs by using feathers and wedges. They each have a rise of 8 inches with a 15-inch tread. A large 8-foot-long marble step was placed at the bottom of the run, parallel with the driveway, to avoid any damage that might be inflicted from cars or snowplows.

INSPIRATIONS

Past …

The ruins of Ollantay tambo (or town) are located about
1 mile (1.6 km) from Machu Picchu, in the Andes mountains
of Peru. The extraordinary stonework of the ancient Incan
people who built these structures is world renowned.

The stones in this
wall located in
Machu Picchu were
cut to a near-perfect
interlocking fit.

... and Present

My neighbor Greg Ford stacked this whimsical stone
piece. In spite of its precarious appearance, the sculpture has proven to be surprisingly stable.

Stone often lends itself to simple designs. This sandstone
table, made with only two stones, adds a true touch of
elegance to the patio of a southwestern home.

With its perfectly centered lichen medallion,
this triangular piece of quartz gneiss stone
makes a beautiful garden ornament.

Function and beauty join hands in this artistic arrangement.
The flat stone is a canvas for delicate shadows and a perch
for resident frogs and migrating birds.

STONE CAIRN

This stone cairn, which I dry-stacked over a period of several weeks, was inspired by the need to make something nonfunctional. Whenever I had a free hour at the end of a day, I unwound by working on this satisfying expression of my appreciation for stone. The rhododendron blooms had vanished before I finished, but the stonework still reflects the seasons. As I write this paragraph, the sculpture is dusted with snow.

Jerry Worley, a local farmer and friend of mine, helped me find the stones; all of them came from his pasture. Jerry also helped me set the very large pedestal stone. Once the pedestal was in place, I decided to stack small, thin stones tightly on top of it to form a central column. To stabilize these stones, I set gravel in the center. Then I made a platform, stepping the stones out slightly to create a spiraling effect. For extra support under portions of the spiral, I inserted wedge stones.

ABOUT THE AUTHOR

Since 1985, David Reed has been working with stone and studying its many uses in the landscape. He shares his love of stone with others by leading workshops in dry-stone building techniques and through his business, The Circle of Stone. He lives in Asheville, North Carolina.

ACKNOWLEDGMENTS

I'd like to thank friends old and new for contributing many beautiful and extraordinary photographs to this book:

Jeff Ashton: pages 13 (top right), 43

David Hildebrand: page 39

Bill Laity, landscaping/construction (Asheville, NC): pages 122, 123 (left), 191

Frederica Lashley: pages 59 (bottom), 121

Leah Leitson, studio potter (Asheville, NC): page 203 (bottom)

Celia Naranjo page 201 (bottom left and right)

Rob Roy: page 25

Ruth Smith, educator: page 203 (top)

Bob Tiller: pages 13 (bottom left), 19 (top left), 29, 106

Rick Woods (Earth Light Photography): page 48

Jane Wooley: pages 40, 46, 47, 49

Stone Carvers

Tom Jackson, Dellrose Artisans, page 11

Jim Morris, page 66 (top)

Stonemasons

Jim MacMillan, Fine Stoneworks Masonry, page 111

David Reed, The Circle of Stone Stonescaping.com, pages 96/97, 101, 107 (left), 182 B

William R. Laity Landscape Company, pages 98, 99, 124, 125

Stone Organizations

Columcille Megalithic Park columcille.org

Dry Stone Conservancy, Inc. DryStoneUSA.org

The Dry Stone Walling Association of Great Britain, dswa.org.uk

Earthwood Building School bigstones.com

Horticulture Center of the Pacific

Stone Foundation, stonefoundation.org

Location Photography

Winterberry Farm, Haywood County, NC

Nelson and Deborah Woodard Delaware Township, NJ

Greg Olson and Rosalind Willis Weaverville, NC

Evan Moquah and Jackie Taylor

Turtle Run Farm, Hot Springs, NC

Martin and Barbara Webster

Starforest Quilts, Burnsville, NC

Richard and Ginger Lang, Crabtree, NC

Marge and Mac Cates, Linville, NC

Sid and Emily Heilbraun Asheville, NC

Clyde and Adrienne Hollifield Black Mountain, NC

Darryl D. Nabors D. D. S., Clyde, NC

Donna Billings and Dennis White Asheville, NC

Chrissie Callejas, Sugar Grove, NC

Judy Carter and Susan Sluyter Wintersun Farm (B&B) Fairview, NC

Marge and Mac Cates, Linville, NC

Marshall and Elizabeth Chapman Linville, NC

Sammy and Candace Cox 4-H Camp, Swannanoa, NC

Jake and Florence Haynes, Linville, NC

Herb Mountain Farm, Weaverville, NC

Peggy Irving, Linville, NC

Lillywhite Stone Farmington, NM

Dick McDonald and Kate Cahow Sugar Grove, NM

Dr. Tom Milton and Ellen Williams Biltmore, NC

The North Carolina Arboretum Asheville, NC

Laurie and Robbie Oates Sugar Grove, NC

Bud Poe and Rebecca Digman Placitias, NM

Dr. Rodney and Laura Pugh Biltmore, NC

Mike and Polly Hutchinson

Casey Farm, Saunders Town, RI

Dave and Elaine Whitehead North Saanich, Vancouver

Robin Hopper and Judi Dyelle Victoria, Vancouver Island, B.C., Canada

Richard Babb, photographer, pages 82 and 83

Thomas Rain Crowe, poet and publisher (New Native Press, Cullowhee, NC), page 1

Bernie K. Digman, photographer, pages 51, 53, 138 (top), 141 (bottom left)

The author's photos appear on pages 32, 33, 53, 54 (center and bottom), 55 (second from top), 56, 57, 71, 72, 73, 74, 77, 79, 85, 86, 87, 88, 133 (right), 136, 140, 141 (bottom right), 155, 164, 165, 169, 170, 175, 183, 186, 188, 193 (top), 194 (top right, bottom), 195 (top right), 199, 201 (top and center rows), 202, (top left and bottom left). Photos of his stonework are shown on pages 53 (right), 73, 85, 189, 194.

SPECIAL THANKS TO

To my parents, Philip and Ann Reed, for their encouragement, enthusiasm, and support; Jackie Taylor, my friend and neighbor, for her creative advice and the loan of her camera equipment; Thomas Rain Crowe, for his photos, the staff at the North Carolina Arboretum and the workshop participants present on the day of the photo shoot; and Scott Lowery, for his beautiful illustrations.

My thanks to Rob Pulleyn for his appreciation of stone and for cheerfully consenting to publish *The Art and Craft of Stonescaping*; Carol Taylor for the opportunity to author *The Art and Craft of Stonework*; Chris Rich and Joe Rhatigan, my editors, for bringing a genuine sense of order and understanding to a mountain of text; Evan Bracken, for his excellent photography and his ability to conjure up clouds when necessary; and Michelle Owen, for adding her splendid sense of aesthetics to the book's pages.

Robbie Oates, stonemason, for writing the section "Trimming Stones for Walls," for his technical assistance and collaboration on many sections of this book, and for his help with location photography. Examples of Robbie's stonework are shown on 62, 142, 174, 184.

Art Garst, landscape designer, Landscaper Gardeners, for his technical assistance and collaboration on the section entitled "Waterfall Pools" and for his help with location photography. Photos of Art's work appear on pages 89, 161, 163, 168, 172, 173, 176.

Chip Smith, soil scientist (Natural Resources Conservation Service, Asheville, NC), for his technical assistance with the "Stone and Gravel" section.

Frederica Lashley, stonemason (The Unturned Stone), for her help with location photography. Examples of her work are on pages 57 and 186.

Lowell Hayes, artist and landscape designer (Hard to Find Gallery, Valle Crucis, NC), for his technical assistance with the section entitled Naturalizing with Stone.

Jim MacMillian, stonemason (Fine Stone Work, Boone, NC), for technical assistance with the sections on paving with stone. His work can be seen on pages 70 and 77.

Jane Wooley of the Dry Stone Conservancy, Dr. Lara Setti, Joe Roberts, Evan Moquah, Anthony Neal, Marjorie Vestal, Tom Boyd, Iris Photographics, Michael Greenfield, Don Fraser, Paul Moore, Amy Burkett, Sam Taylor, Nancy Reed, Paul Arnold, and Andrea Latier.

GALLERY STONEMASON BIOS

Marc Archambault is a strong believer in the sustainability in stonework construction and an advocate of building without mortar or concrete. Using old-school masonry techniques, Marc enjoys creating complex natural stone mosaics. He lives in Asheville, North Carolina, and maintains an active website and blog, hammerheadstoneworks.com.

Alan Ash is a Master Stonemason in Eugene, Oregon. Alan works with both dry-laid and mortared masonry. He teaches classes for the University of Oregon School of Architecture's Northwest Preservation Field School as well as Oregon State Parks. He holds an Instructor's Certificate from Great Britain's Dry Stone Walling Association. Find out more about Alan's work at thestonemason.com.

Joe Dinwiddie is qualified at the Intermediate level by the Dry Stone Walling Association and leads many educational programs and workshops on drystone masonry. His business, Dinwiddie Drystone Masonry, is located in Black Mountain, North Carolina. Visit drystonejoe.com to see more of his work.

Chuck Eblacker is a dry-stone waller and one of only a handful of Americans who has earned an advanced certificate from the Dry Stone Walling Association of Great Britain. He lives in Rochester, New York. To see a portfolio of Chuck's projects, visit Eblackerstone.com.

Matt Goddard hand selects the materials for each of his projects. Each stone's color and form plays a key part in the creation of his attractive installations. Matt lives in Corbett, Oregon, and documents his work at Poetryinstone.com.

Jason Hoffman is a professional dry-stone waller based in Livingston, Scotland. More of his work is available for view at stoneinspired.com.

Mark Jurus, from Hampstead, Maryland, specializes in the craft of dry-laid stone construction. He carries dual certifications from the Dry Stone Conservancy USA and the Dry Stone Walling Association of Great Britain. To see more documented projects, visit his blog/website at Rockinwalls.com.

David Findlay Wilson of Perth, United Kingdom, is a public artist that works with stone as well as metal. Many of his projects are created using traditional craftsmanship with a modern aesthetic. His innovative design and inspirational use of stone at the Edinburgh Airport Interchange won him the Dry Stone Walling Association of Great Britain's Pinnacle Award. You can see more examples of David's work at dfwilson.co.uk.

*Bold type indicates main reference

Withdrawn

SEP 1 6 2024

Public Library of
St Joe County